ADVENTURERS

HUAWEI STORIES

TIAN TAO
YIN ZHIFENG

Published by
LID Publishing Limited
The Record Hall, Studio 304,
16-16a Baldwins Gardens,
London EC1N 7RJ, UK

info@lidpublishing.com
www.lidpublishing.com

A member of:

businesspublishersroundtable.com

© Huawei Investment & Holding Co., Ltd. 2020
© LID Publishing Limited, 2020

Printed by CPI Group (UK) Ltd, Croydon CR0 4YY
ISBN: 978-1-911671-02-2
ISBN: 978-1-911671-36-7 (ebook)

Cover and page design: Caroline Li

ADVENTURERS

HUAWEI STORIES

TIAN TAO
YIN ZHIFENG

MADRID | MEXICO CITY | LONDON
NEW YORK | BUENOS AIRES
BOGOTA | SHANGHAI | NEW DELHI

Contents

Preface

Becoming the World's Best-Loved Smart Device Brand

By Richard Yu

Victory or death for Huawei's Consumer Business Group

In October 2011, a three-day workshop was held at Sanya, Hainan Province. Attended by all Huawei executives and specialist domain experts, this workshop focused on discussing Huawei's strategy in the consumer electronics business. The debate was intense. Most attendees had worked in the business-to-business (B2B) market for years, and it was difficult for them to agree on a path through the issues in this brand-new business-to-consumer (B2C) space. However, everyone agreed on one thing: Huawei must become a major player in the consumer electronics space. But back then, no company in the world had ever succeeded in both the B2B and B2C domains.

On 15 December 2011, Huawei's founder and CEO, Mr Ren Zhengfei, signed off on the Sanya resolution. This resolution laid out our principles for the consumer business, and said that Huawei's competitiveness in this space begins and ends with consumers. Many of us were deeply inspired by the huge opportunities in front of us and the historic mission on our shoulders.

That same year, I stepped down as Huawei's Chief Strategy and Marketing Officer in order to fully devote myself to the consumer business. Our team set a goal: "If we decide to enter a domain, then we will strive to become the leader in that domain." We wanted consumers to see that the world's best mobile phones could come from Huawei.

Competitiveness begins and ends with consumers

When I joined Huawei as a fresh graduate in 1993, Huawei was still a very small company. At my new employee orientation meeting, Mr Ren told us, "Huawei will become the best communications company in the world." My colleagues and I thought this would be impossible to achieve. When we started to develop Huawei's own consumer device brand in 2011, we set the challenging goal of selling one million premium Huawei-branded smartphones. Everyone thought this was an impossible goal.

Over the years, two words could sum up the Consumer Business Group (BG) experience: hard work. Everything has been difficult. Despite this, our seemingly impossible targets have been achieved one by one. We experienced bumpy beginnings, gradual overtaking and high-speed growth. And this is all because our company chose and stuck to the harder path.

Huawei's consumer business started in 2003. We are in the tele-coms business, and our first product was a simple communications tool: fixed wireless terminals for remote villages. We gave many people in remote areas access to communications services for the first time. In the next few years, we became the global number one in 3G dongles. Between 2003 and 2010, our outstanding performance in fixed wireless terminals and dongles ensured our survival. We entered the mobile phone market with a white label strategy, where we served as an original design manufacturer (ODM) for telecom operators. This enabled us to gain experience in phone manufactur-ing and laid a solid foundation for our subsequent move from the B2B domain to the B2C domain.

In 2012, Huawei's consumer business officially started a three-pronged strategic shift: from white label to Huawei-branded; from low-end phones to mid-range and high-end smartphones; and from telecom operator resale to the open market. At the time, some media outlets did not see consumer electronics as a good move for Huawei. In fact, they called us crazy.

We weren't crazy, but we were radical. Our research and devel-opment (R&D) team made its largest ever investment. Every sin-gle person in every single process threw themselves into the new endeavour with utter commitment. We wanted to transform our-selves and occupy the high-end market. We would do whatever it took to shave just a fraction of a millimetre off our phone, to deliver the best possible experiences to our customers.

Our radical approach finally paid off. In 2012, we launched our first flagship smartphone, the HUAWEI P1, which was quickly recognized as the world's thinnest smartphone. This phone had an incredible design and was highly competitive. However, Huawei had almost zero experience in branding, sales channels or retail. With a price tag of ¥3,000, this phone was targeted at the high-end segment, but did not sell very well. This was the first lesson we learned in the B2C sector.

On the positive side, consumers were amazed to see that Huawei, a company known for being the home of geeky engineers, could actually deliver a product with flair and style. The positive feedback from consumers gave us tremendous confidence, and our determi-nation to succeed in the consumer sector was stronger than ever.

In 2012, we cut our planned production of 50 million feature phones to 20 million units, and fully committed ourselves to smartphones. During this transition period, the consumer team faced seemingly impossible challenges. We had to deal with the backlash from telecom operators as a result of our reduced feature phone production plan, and it was difficult for us to quickly gain a foothold in the high-end market due to our lack of experience in building a B2C brand. In spite of these difficulties, Huawei continued to increase its investment in the R&D of smart devices. In particular, we continued to innovate in the premium smartphone segment.

At the beginning of 2013, I applied for a "Starting from Zero" Award from the company, meaning that I would receive a year-end bonus of zero for 2012. Even though we had actually hit our targets for 2012, I wanted to use this award to 'motivate' my team and myself. We have to put ourselves in a position where there is only one way out, and then achieve it with complete determination. That is the only way to launch ourselves to greater things. I still have the "Starting from Zero" Award on my desk today. It is a model of the J-15 Flying Shark – China's first generation of fighter configured to land on an aircraft carrier – taking off from the *Liaoning*.

In 2014, Huawei's branding strategy for our consumer business was rewritten. Honor was originally the name of one of our device models. We decided to promote it to an independent business unit that would target a specific group of consumers, and would have the freedom to innovate and grow rapidly. Our Honor brand was to become an online retailer, and to that end, all of our separate online sales teams in the consumer business were combined into one platform.

Since then, the Huawei brand and Honor brand have developed side by side, combining to create synergy. Honor is committed to delivering stylish new tech for the younger generation. The Huawei brand focuses on innovative features and a superior experience, and aims to expand our share in the high-end market and serve a wider audience.

It has been more than seven years since we expanded into the B2C market. Changing our own mindset has always been our biggest weakness. In the past, I tended to shy away from the media. Later, I forced myself to advertise Huawei on social media every day.

Over the past few years, all Consumer BG managers have been required to get out on the front lines and regularly sell our products and provide services in retail stores, so that they engage directly with our customers and hear their feedback. We have sent open letters to all employees, calling on them to represent Huawei to their family and friends. Every employee in our Consumer BG should be able to answer questions about Huawei products and our customers' end-to-end experience with our devices.

In the beginning, the key elements of our core strategy for the consumer business were: building premium products; creating a solid brand; and building sales channels and retail experience. This strategy evolved as time went on, and we incorporated new elements such as our dual brand strategy (Huawei and Honor), user engagement, ecosystem building and value chain integration. In this way we have built up our consumer segment operations step by step.

The journey was not an easy one. We have experienced many frustrations, pains and struggles. At the most difficult moments, the understanding and support shown by Mr Ren and other members of the Huawei senior management team gave us the determination and courage to continue the transformation. We firmly believed that if we could survive the transition, Huawei's Consumer BG would become bigger and stronger. We are a marathon runner, in it for the long haul.

Huawei already had powerful business and operational systems that were developed for our telecom equipment business over the years, and we were able to use these systems to quickly make up for any shortcomings and become a leader in the areas of software and hardware R&D, communications capabilities, supply chain, manufacturing and chipsets. We gradually built up unique strengths that set us apart from the competition.

Huawei's in-house Kirin chips were not well regarded when they first appeared in 2012, but they have now become one of our strengths as a product developer. Awareness of the Huawei brand was less than 3% in our home country of China at the beginning of our journey, but by 2017, global brand awareness was 86%. This means that nearly nine in every ten people around the world know the Huawei name.

In 2014, Huawei became the first company on the Chinese mainland to appear in Interbrand's Best Global Brands list,[1] having secured the 94th spot. Our ranking moved up to 70th place several years later. In 2017, Honor became the number one online-only Chinese mobile phone brand by sales volume and revenue.

Since 2015, Huawei has cemented its position as one of the top three smartphone manufacturers in the world. Our smartphone shipments in 2018 are expected to top 200 million units, almost placing us in second place for global market share. We are the top seller in China and several other markets. Our market share in China is over 30%, and in the high-end smartphone segment (smartphones priced over ¥4,000), Huawei and Apple are the only two competitors left.

We are keenly aware that our achievements would not have been possible without the trust and support of our customers. We have also realized that, as we continue to progress, we must maintain a sense of respect and humility around customer experience and customer satisfaction. Over the years, Huawei employees have put our customers at the heart of everything we do and have never given up. This fighting spirit has brought us to where we are today, and will continue to drive us forward as we step into the future.

The only limit is our own ambition

The more ambitious our goals are, the better results we will achieve.

Our team has always believed that we must have lofty aspirations and vision. To me, having vision means many things. In addition to ambition, it also means inclusiveness, willpower and seeing the big picture. Being a winner is a question of attitude: we must always aim to be the best, and everything we do must be done well. And our managers must have a deep understanding of our business and profound strategic insight. They must climb higher and see further than our competitors.

When I was the president of Huawei's Wireless Network Product Line more than ten years ago, our team had a clear goal: beat all competitors. With this goal in mind, we boldly innovated and made breakthroughs, and developed the world's first distributed base station and the SingleRAN[2] range, making our products the best in the world. More than a decade has passed since then, and those products are still second to none in the industry.

Over the years, we have gradually built up our own strengths in consumer electronics in the areas of smartphone battery life, communications capabilities, cameras and Android optimization. In some areas, we are the world leader. More importantly, we have gradually built a consumer team that is focused and hard-working, pursues ambitious goals and faces challenges head-on. Strategy is important, but a well-functioning team is more important to our success. How a team looks and operates, all the way from the top to the bottom, determines how far it can go in the future.

Our strategy is to deliver an intelligent experience to consumers across all scenarios by providing them with smartphones, tablets, PCs, wearables, health and fitness services, smart home services and connected vehicle services:

- Thanks to our years of sustained investment in R&D, Huawei has gone from an unknown brand in the tablet market to being the third largest player globally
- As a new entrant in the PC market, Huawei has won acclaim from consumers for multiple innovations. The HUAWEI MateBook series has made a mark in the high-end PC market
- In the first quarter of 2018, our wearables led the industry with a year-on-year growth rate of nearly 150%. Our smart watches have achieved a number of industry firsts over the past several years
- We have been working hard in the connected vehicle domain, with annual shipments exceeding 10 million units. We are leading the industry, serving 15 well-known automobile brands around the world
- This year, our HiLink ecosystem will offer more than 400 smart home appliance products across more than 70 categories. The HiLink protocol is becoming a mainstream international standard

In the smart home and smart city domains, our device chipsets have grown by leaps and bounds. We have gone from being a new player to a leader in multiple fields. We have become a major supplier of chipsets for global video surveillance devices, smart home devices, and Internet of Things (IoT) devices. In the mobile broadband market, Huawei will maintain its decade-long absolute leadership in 3G and 4G in the 5G era. We are the industry pacesetter.

A fully connected, intelligent world is around the corner. In this world, we will innovate and make breakthroughs in the areas of artificial intelligence (AI), cloud services, screens, storage, cameras and chipsets through greater chip–device–cloud synergy. In addition, we will continue to take security and privacy protection very seriously, and will develop the capabilities needed to protect our smart devices and users. Our goal is to deliver a secure, inspired, intelligent experience to consumers the world over, regardless of how they use their devices.

However, we are well aware that we still have a long way to go in the areas of retail, sales channels, branding, processes and IT systems if we want to become number one in the smart device industry. We must identify our weaknesses by benchmarking ourselves against the top players in the industry. Then we can constantly innovate, surpass our competitors, and surpass ourselves. If we are able to build a world-class team in each domain, then we will undoubtedly become the world's top company.

Huawei must strive to develop the world's best products by focusing everything we do on our consumers. Nobody remembers second best.

Working together with the best people

Talent has always been our most valuable asset. We will continue with our elite team strategy, and deploy the world's best resources, tools, methods and people so that we can become the world leader.

The high-speed growth of our consumer business over the past several years is largely attributable to the concentrated efforts of the many managers and engineers who were assigned to us from different departments across the company every year. Huawei's more than 100,000 employees are united in their goals and aligned in their incentives, and they have helped make us what we are today. The wealth of experience gathered by the company within our business and operational systems provides a solid foundation for the development of our consumer business.

We would like to thank the company for giving us the freedom to operate as a relatively independent unit, allowing us to respond to the rhythm and logic of the B2C market. We are thus able to manage our end-to-end processes ranging from R&D and sales to marketing, services, supply chain and finance. We have developed a complete set of processes and IT support systems for the B2C business. Thus our operations are practised and well-planned, and our business is much more efficient. As a part of the Huawei family, we share Huawei's goals and values: we help our customers succeed by staying consumer-centric, and we manage our brand with integrity.

We will continue with our elite team strategy. We attract outstanding people from the world's most exciting talent hubs, in order to build an open and inclusive team that balances a wide range of different skillsets. We are always looking for the brightest, and we hope that every bold, intelligent and passionate person will join and work alongside us. Our team will become the best business team in the world!

There will be a shakeout of the smart device industry over the next three to five years, 2021–2023. We strongly believe that Huawei will be one of the two or three global phone brands to survive the crunch, and one of the very few mainstream phone makers to survive in China. In fact, we will not just survive; we will thrive. In 2014 and 2015, we fought for survival and managed to keep our head above water. In 2016 and 2017, we fought for a global position, and have basically achieved this goal. In 2018, the three-camera technology on our new HUAWEI P20 Pro offered customers a revolutionary camera experience and delivered a clear edge in terms of battery life, communications capabilities and charging speed. Our P20 phones have become bestsellers around the world, and we are set to continue launching more disruptive products and innovative technologies onto the global market: 2018 will be the first year in which we set foot on the path to true global pre-eminence.

This team came together in the consumer business because of our common cause. In the Consumer BG, we have developed and we experience a brand with warmth and a team with heat. Here, we "toast those who succeed and offer a helping hand to those who fail." What can keep us together in the Consumer BG, aside from just money? One thing is great career opportunities. But what I cherish more are the close relationships we have forged in our team. The feeling that everyone here is like family helps us to stay committed, stay practical and keep enjoying ourselves.

The people who change the world are those who have great dreams and work hard to realize those dreams. To realize great dreams, we have to bring together a group of dedicated people. Always keep consumers in mind, and always prioritize improving the consumer experience and creating consumer value. Have the courage to innovate, make breakthroughs and lead, and work relentlessly to achieve all of these things. This is the unique DNA of our consumer team, and I firmly believe that a better future belongs to those who have this passion coursing through their veins.

Huawei's consumer business has taken more than ten years to become what it is today. This would not have been possible without the dedication and hard work of Huawei employees over the years. Behind the scenes, there have been many stories about our blood, sweat and tears, as well as our joy and success. We have put together a few of these stories and would like to share them with you.

We would like to dedicate this book to all of the Huawei fans out there, our partners, our friends from the media and all of the customers around the world who have stuck with us along the way. We would also like to express our most sincere gratitude to every Huawei colleague who has worked, is working and will continue to work closely with us, and your loved ones.

Our mission is to make Huawei the first choice and the most trusted smart device brand in the world. We will do everything we can to achieve this mission.

Shenzhen
July 2018

---

1   Interbrand is a brand consulting firm. Established in 1974, the company has published its Best Global Brands list since 2000. The rankings measure a brand from three areas: (1) the financial performance of the branded products or services; (2) the role the brand plays in purchase decisions; and (3) the brand's competitive strength and its ability to create loyalty and, therefore, sustainable demand and profit into the future.

2   SingleRAN is a radio access network (RAN) technology offered by Huawei that allows mobile telecommunications operators to support multiple mobile communications standards and wireless telephone services on a single network. The technology incorporates a software-defined radio device, and is designed with a consolidated set of hardware components, allowing operators to purchase, operate and maintain a single telecommunications network and set of equipment.

Why Leica?

By Li Changzhu

It has been said that mobile phones disrupted the camera industry. But one camera maker is an intimate part of the Huawei story.

A camera is a must-have function for any modern phone. And when one phone is compared against another, the quality of cameras is one of the key indicators. Every phone maker is busy deploying technologies to make the best phone camera. Very quickly, dramatic improvements have been made in image quality, with pixel counts, high definition, filters, optical image stabilization, selfie editors and night shooting modes ... These options have also given users a much richer photography experience. Today, we no longer have to drag a heavy camera around with us. A phone is all we need to capture every highlight and precious memory.

Huawei believes that the digital era has not fundamentally changed the world we live in. A rose by any other name would smell as sweet, and a phone camera is still a camera. The principles of image capture, optics and picture quality control have never changed. If we want to give phone users exceptional picture quality and a good camera experience, then we have to focus our own attention on the fundamentals of photography. Huawei is always thinking about how a phone can reproduce the great photos of the film era. How can photos taken on your phone have emotion and meaning, in the way that the old great photographers managed? Our research took us to the doorstep of one of the greatest companies in the camera industry, and its name is Leica.

Why Leica?

Among photographers, Leica is a legendary company. The designer Oskar Barnack made the prototype Ur-Leica camera, which used 35 mm motion picture film, by hand in 1914. This was the world's first portable camera. But even more important than that, over the following century, Leica maintained a tradition of excellence. Many great photographers have used Leica cameras to capture some of their greatest moments. From Robert Capa's *Falling Soldier* to *V-J Day in Times Square*, from the portrait of Zhou Enlai to the victory pose of Muhammad Ali, Leica cameras have been faithful witnesses to history.

The key to Leica's brilliance has always been in their optical systems. Leica lenses are produced through a process of extraordinary complexity. They use unique raw materials and, in order to smooth out any internal tension within the lenses, the optical glass in each lens must be allowed to cool over a gradual, slow process that can take months. The village of Wetzlar, home to Leica, is known as Europe's Silicon Valley for optics. Generations of optics experts have spent their careers here, experimenting, altering and designing. Leica images are sharp, the colours saturated and the tones lucid. Subjects stand out sharply from their backgrounds. The high resolving power of the lens gives images great depth of field and Leica's signature glossiness.

Over the course of a century, Leica has developed its own unique culture. Its new cameras have never disappointed camera enthusiasts: every detail is polished to perfection. Leica cameras have become a symbol of professionalism. They represent a guarantee of creative thought, as an extension of photographers' own sense of vision. In addition, their high price has always meant that Leica cameras are a byword for luxury.

Using a Leica camera is the pursuit of taste and culture. Leica makes cameras to be used for life. At the launch of the iPhone 4, Steve Jobs used Leica as his own comparison for quality: "This is, beyond doubt, one of the most precise and beautiful things we've ever made. It's like a beautiful old Leica camera."

Could a matchup between Huawei and the venerable Leica generate new sparks of excitement?

Companies with chemistry

The first time Huawei visited Leica was in the summer of 2014. Contact started back in late 2013, when Huawei established email contact with Leica, and suggested that the companies work together. During that first contact, Leica politely turned Huawei down. But after a few more email exchanges, Leica eventually agreed to meet with Huawei.

The first meeting began with a visit to the Leica plant. The centenary of Leica's founding fell in 2014, and the company had just moved into its new headquarters. From the air, the headquarters is a mass of round and double-barrelled motifs, symbolizing Leica's two main businesses: binoculars and cameras.

In the lobby of the new headquarters there is a small gallery open to the public, where Leica keeps a permanent display of photographers' work. This was where I first saw the whole range of Leica cameras up close, and it was the first time I realized that so many famous images had originally been captured by Leica cameras. Here, I first saw the Leica M Monochrom, the digital camera that earned headlines for only taking black and white photographs.

The lobby connects straight to the factory behind. Visitors can observe the lens production and assembly lines. When we visited, though, there was not a single person in the entire production facility. It turned out that Germany was playing their first World Cup match that afternoon, so everyone had gone home to watch the game, with the exception of the CEO and the manager who met with us. It just goes to show how important football is in Germany!

During that first meeting, Huawei and Leica both gave presentations on our two companies. The CEO himself spent 20 minutes listening to our presentation. We agreed to take what we had learned back home to our company leadership. Leica would do the same, and we would push for a second meeting.

Just those two hours at Leica filled me with admiration for the company. The company represents a century of creating high-quality images. From the start, they have been committed to high technology, precision engineering and perfection in the details. Their corporate culture is one of utter focus and perfectionism. In this way, they share their DNA with Huawei. If Huawei could work with Leica on our phone cameras, how might our two companies react together?

Within Leica, there was also a lot of anticipation. Their company had steadily rising sales and very decent profit margins, but the senior leadership were thinking of the future. Leica's mission was to bring high-quality imaging to the world's consumers. In a world where more and more photographs were being taken on smartphones, how could a camera company stay relevant? How could they integrate their century of experience into a smartphone? They would need a diligent strategic partner, with whom they share a vision and technological excellence.

Leica was seeking a partner, and it was at that moment that Huawei came knocking.

Fate is a powerful force. A young technology company from China, and a traditional, century-old German firm. But once we locked eyes, it was an immediate match. We were two companies with chemistry!

Huawei and Leica both approached the relationship with a positive frame of mind. We both stepped out of our comfort zones to understand the other company, and to respect their needs and values. There were meetings at the leadership level, as well. The Leica CEO flew out to Shanghai to meet his Huawei partners. Face to face with the CEO of Huawei's Consumer BG, he was able to negotiate several tricky details and accelerate the pace of our agreement. After several rounds of assessments and negotiations, we were able to sign the strategic partnership agreement. It was very much like starting a relationship: we talked, got to know each other, developed mutual trust, came to an agreement and, finally, were able to join hands. Every step was natural.

The darkest night before the dawn

However, reaching the collaboration agreement was only the first step in a long process. Our goal in working together was to deliver an entirely new photography experience to users, and to give a qualitative boost to the image of Huawei phones. One of the first actions of the companies was to set up a technical expert group. It was led by Dr Weiler from Leica and Dr Yi from Huawei's Consumer BG. The group was given the responsibility for optical design and image quality.

A mobile phone may be small, but it packs in a lot of functions. A phone camera contains every part of a digital camera, though many of the parts are miniaturized. However, there are natural limitations in the optical design of a phone camera. A plastic lens does not give the same optical performance as a glass lens. Some aspects of traditional lens design cannot be reproduced in such a small space. The processing of lens modules is more difficult, and factors such as production cost, ability to mass produce and process yield come into play. So, when Leica presented its optical design standards for lens modules, many problems became obvious immediately.

How would we lift the process yield on these modules?

The design of optical systems had to balance high, medium and low frequencies so that the images would have the required level of detail, depth and clarity. The Leica experts also set high standards for eliminating lens flare and ghosting. Lens flare and ghosting happen when strong light enters the lens, and are caused by multiple reflections within the lens, and they result in a shadow like a skull (ghosting) or bright spots on the image (flare). Flare and ghosting are generally minimized through well-designed optical systems. When Leica explained its testing practices to Huawei and to our suppliers, we were stunned. The light source that Leica used in its tests was as bright as the light of a projector. It was dozens of times brighter than the lights that we typically used for testing. But this extreme testing could completely expose all of the flaws in our optical systems where lens flare and ghosting could be generated. Leica insisted on checking our phone lens units with the same standards of tests that it used for Leica lenses, because good lenses are fundamental to excellent image capture.

On the first few runs, our process yields were dismal. For every 100 lenses we produced, fewer than ten two-lens units passed quality tests. The optical technology team and the engineers of 2012 Labs took on this challenge together. And the final results proved, beyond a shadow of a doubt, that Huawei engineers are uncompromising in their pursuit of excellence. There is always a solution to be found, and we worked shoulder to shoulder with our suppliers and with the Leica experts until we had resolved each and every difficulty.

Leica's experts often came with us to our suppliers' production facilities so that we could discuss the best solutions together. They gave us the full benefit of their long experience in the design and manufacturing of optical systems, guiding us in how to adjust the shape of the lenses and the distances between them, and how to take the interactions between optical units and other systems into consideration. We all worked to improve the situation, and over time the process yield improved. Finally, on the project due date, we reached the standard that we needed to shift to mass production.

During the test runs for each batch of lenses, many sample photos had to be taken to assess the image quality. On one occasion, Leica's experts compared the sample photos taken using our phones with those taken by a top phone brand. The results made the experts dance a jig, because our lens had hit the levels required for first-class quality.

The lenses for the P9 and P9 Plus were true Leica lenses. They were part of the Summarit series, with an aperture of 2.2–2.5 mm. Everyone can try this for themselves: point the phone toward a bright light source and take a photo. You will find almost no lens flare or ghosting, just a soft halo with well-controlled transitions from bright to dark areas. With a little adjustment, you can capture a very nice backlight image.

How to capture that Leica essence in a photo

Huawei's image quality experts realized that even when both Huawei and Leica were using the same equipment and system to test images, Leica was applying much more stringent standards. For example, when we used the colour chart to test colour accuracy, we would test a few dozen colour patches. Leica was checking every single one of the 140 colour patches on the chart. To reach Leica's required levels of quality, Huawei had to set standards that take in not just the lens, but other phone components, the image signal processing algorithms and the post-processing.

The tests for image quality included colour, focus, texture, noise, distortion and movement. Completing all of these tests was a major project in itself. The tests came in two parts: objective and subjective. The objective indicators were quantitative, with tests designed to be entirely replicable. The subjective assessment looked at common photographic subjects. Huawei's multimedia R&D department had a team that specialized in image quality assessments, and they already had more than 100 different types of typical photo subjects, as well as incidental subjects.

The image testing team spent their days taking sample photos, and collecting large numbers of beta test shots to find and analyse any problems within them. Some members of the testing team ended up working virtually around the clock. Whether the sample photos came in from the US or from Europe, they always scrambled to give us a solution as quickly as possible. Just imagine dealing with so many questions day after day, every question needing its own follow-up and solution. This was tough work, but they were a tough team, and ready for the job. I was a pretty experienced team member, too. I was out with the HUAWEI P9 taking photos every day from January to February 2016. With every upgrade, I could see the quality of the pictures improving. We were advancing, step by step, toward that Leica essence. It took the commitment of every team member, discovering problems, solving problems, round and round, over and over, but never giving up.

Light at the end of the tunnel

On 3 April 2016, Huawei unveiled the P9 and the P9 Plus to an audience of more than 1,500 journalists in London, representing hundreds of different outlets and publications from all over the world. The highlight that day was clearly the Leica-supported dual lens camera. At the launch, we had four respected international photographers present the pictures that they had captured using the P9 and share their experiences when using the P9 camera.

On 15 April Huawei's Consumer BG CEO, Richard Yu, launched the P9 to Chinese consumers in Shanghai. Leica's CEO and other executives spoke at the launch. The phone hit the shelves of retail stores in China at 6 pm that night.

I found that more and more of my friends were buying the HUAWEI P9, and I made new friends through the new phone. The P9 had a series of surprises in store for them.

Some friends found the P9's monochrome mode to be particularly cool. They were able to take black and white photos brimming with that crisp Leica essence. Of course, one of the two P9 cameras is a dedicated black and white lens. It serves as a standalone black and white camera, as well as working in concert with the other lens to recognize image depth, capture extra detail and reduce noise. Leica's century of experience finding the perfect focus for black and white photographs is now embodied not just in the M Monochrom, but also in the P9.

How can photos taken
on your phone have
emotion and meaning
in the way that the old great
photographers managed?

Second-hand books taken with a HUAWEI P20 Pro (wide aperture)

Other friends fell in love with the P9's wide aperture effect. The P9 had two lenses and a laser rangefinder, so it was able to generate detailed information on the depth of the subject scene. This makes it possible to adjust the focus and the depth of the shot algorithmically. Even though it's done with algorithms, the glossy softness and the bokeh effect outside the focal zone provide the perfect backdrop to emphasize the main subject. This is a camera effect that photographers love and return to again and again.

Some Leica fans have found that using the P9 is a strangely familiar experience. This is because Huawei and Leica engineers worked together on the design of the P9's user interface. Many of the operations and menus are the same as those in the Leica M series; the font used is the same as Leica's and even the shutter sound is the same.

Many people wonder just how it was that Leica and Huawei came together – one a high-class luxury brand, the other a maker of consumer electronics. Wouldn't there be some clash in their design approaches? After the launch of the P9 and P9 Plus, a reporter put this question to the CEO of Leica, who offered a very candid answer: we think that Huawei products are of premium quality, in terms of selection of raw materials, use of the most advanced technologies, and Huawei's quality standards for software and hardware. All of these reflect a high-class product. Leica has a century-old brand name, and is very protective of its name. It puts a lot of thought into the selection of its partners, and is extremely cautious. But ultimately it selected Huawei to be its long-term strategic partner for smart devices.

Exactly what advances did Huawei and Leica make?

Mobile phones are now universal, and more and more people are using them to record the details of their lives, and capture moments with personal meaning. These photographs make up the world in their eyes. They are a record of their real world. People are increasingly used to using photographs as a third mode of communication and self-expression, a new addition to voice and text communications. All of these fragmentary images of ordinary people make up the rich texture of global progress and social change. We use our phones to take pictures, but at the same time we are making a record of history. The quick snaps we take today will become a part of the historical record in a few years' time. Looking back at our own photos generates a sense of closeness and lived experience that is quite unique.

That is why Huawei and Leica's partnership is not just about technology. It is an evolution from a phone camera to phone photography, a leap from quick snaps to expression and emotion. What Huawei and Leica together give to users is a photographic story with a real emotional connection, self-expression with real human content and human engagement with warmth and connection. We create high-quality products and build an emotional connection with our users. That has always been our shared goal and vision.

There is much more to look forward to in the future of Huawei phone photography.

The Secret to Zero Dropped Calls

By Huang Xuewen

The high-speed train was travelling at more than 300 km/h from Beijing to Shanghai. But one businessman couldn't wait to reach his destination. He grabbed his luggage and got off the train halfway through his journey in Jinan, so that he could finally dial in to an important conference call. The poor reception on the train meant that his call kept being dropped, and the only way to stay in on the call was to abandon his trip.

In 2016, I met this man as we carried out a market survey, and he told me his story. He explained that he would often travel between Beijing and Shanghai, and bitterly complained about the weak signal on the high-speed trains. Many people listening nodded their heads in agreement, obviously having had similar experiences themselves:

I chose to travel by train instead of by air because I thought I would be able to make that phone call. If I had known about the terrible signal quality on the trains, I wouldn't have bothered.

Now, I don't even want to look at my phone on the train.

I wonder if anyone can fix this issue and improve the signal on these trains.

When he realized that I was responsible for mobile communications quality at Huawei, he approached me and said, "I know Huawei isn't directly responsible for signal quality on trains. But Huawei has 30 years of experience in the carrier business, and you're doing well in the smartphone market, too. Isn't there something you can do?"

When I told my colleagues about this encounter, they shared my determination: whatever our customers' problems are, it's our job to fix them. One thing this customer said resonated with us: through 30 years of experience, Huawei had indeed developed a unique understanding of the best technology in the wireless network business, as well as strength in smartphone research and development. So, even though we were not technically in charge of mobile coverage on trains, we decided to try and solve the issue in our own way.

A high-speed train in the lab

We decided to start with the busiest railway line in China, which runs between Beijing and Shanghai. The Consumer BG established a joint project team to focus on improving our users' phone experience on high-speed trains. We brought together an all-star line-up from the consumer team, the wireless network team, and HiSilicon, Huawei's chipset design unit.

The team's first job was to determine the root cause of the issue. Why was mobile coverage so poor on trains? How could we improve it? We certainly couldn't take all kinds of bulky testing equipment and camp out on the train. The line between Beijing and Shanghai is over 1,000 km long; each round trip would take almost a full day. This would have clearly been a cumbersome and inefficient way to proceed. Luckily, we were able to get help from one of Huawei's secret weapons instead – the Device Communications Instrument Testing Centre.

Built at a cost of over ¥200 million, this high-tech testing centre delivers quality testing and certification for 14 leading global telecom operators. The centre has been certified by the China National Accreditation Service for Conformity Assessment, and its work has been validated and recognized by leading institutions such as the Global Certification Forum (GCF), AT&T, China Mobile and China Telecom.

The centre has a virtual field-testing system that is among the best in the industry. This meant we would only have to go out and collect the data and parameters that we might need, and then input these into the testing system, which could then run simulations with high accuracy. Careful analysis would help us discover the root cause behind the weak signal strength on trains.

Mr Tang, from the Consumer BG, led a crew to the site to collect data. For a period of about seven days you could have seen us every day on the Beijing–Shanghai train, sitting with an assembly of computers and mobile phones made by all different companies. Each day we rode back and forth to conduct uninterrupted call testing along the entire length of the line. We brought back 400 GB of data and samples of dropped calls.

Testing on the high-speed train

With the data we collected, we built a 'high-speed train' in our lab. By entering the data into our system, we were able to simulate different frequency bands and radio access technologies all along the railway, including all the places where the signal suddenly got weaker or stronger. We could now connect any mobile phone to the system, and it would respond just as if it were on the train, racing along in the analogue world. This system was like taking a CT scan of a patient in the hospital. It allowed us to see exactly where the pain was.

Phone, chipset and network in perfect harmony

We identified two main causes of weak signal on high-speed trains.

The first was poor network coverage. This was easy to understand. The railway runs through some remote, sparsely populated areas with complex terrain between the cities of Cangzhou and Dezhou, for example. When the train passed through these areas, there simply wasn't much signal to connect to, and so there were frequent dropped calls.

The second reason was a little more complicated. Mobile phone signals naturally vary all the time. First, I'll explain the situation along the railway line. China's three major telecom operators all have networks covering the whole line from Beijing to Shanghai. Each network is made up of cells, each cell covering a certain area and slightly overlapping with its neighbours. This is what 'cellular network' means.

We had worked for many years with the telecom operators, so we were able to dig out more detailed data. There were about 350 cells along the line from Beijing to Shanghai, and the Fuxing high-speed train could complete the journey in about 250 minutes. On average, it would switch from one cell to the next every 40 seconds. For one third of the cells, the train stayed in the cell for less than 30 seconds.

We also found that over 80% of the dropped calls happened when the train was crossing between two neighbouring cells. You can imagine the phone as a relay baton, repeatedly being handed from one cell to the next as it flies across the cells. The faster the train went, the less time the cells had to prepare for each handover, and that meant a higher probability of dropping the call.

It seemed like the dropped calls had nothing to do with phones themselves. So why did we even care? Well, we had to. We had amassed such extensive experience building networks for telecom operators over so many years. As long as there was a chance that we could improve customers' experience, we had to try.

First, we addressed the poor network coverage. We identified the locations along the railway where the most dropped calls happened for each of the three telecom operators' services – China Mobile, China Telecom and China Unicom. Our wireless experts then reached out to these operators and discussed potential solutions with them. This involved the operators updating their network parameters in some places or optimizing their networks in others. Soon, the mobile networks of all three operators significantly improved all along the Beijing–Shanghai line. Improving the networks helped improve call quality for all phones. It was a small contribution that we could make to improve the experience for all passengers travelling on this line.

The second problem was a little more difficult. Resolving it was beyond the ability of the operators. We changed our tactics here and thought that we might be able to solve the network problems from the phone side. We considered adding a new feature to our mobile chipsets and, given Huawei's ability to develop chipsets, we believed we could certainly crack the problem. We had worked with the HiSilicon team before, and knew that they would respond quickly to any request to improve customer experience. We saved a lot of time by working with Huawei phones, as ours use in-house chipsets. This avoided a lot of lengthy back and forth with outside vendors.

After multiple rounds of intense discussion, and going over every possible solution, we finally agreed on a method that would allow mobile phones to tell in advance when a switch to another cell was about to take place. Big data was key in this solution. We analysed massive lakes of traffic data from each cell along the line to work out the cells where phones perform best. Then we looked at the phones, because physical infrastructure takes a long time to change, but the phone can be updated easily. For any given stretch of track, there might be five or six cells, or signals, that a phone could connect with. That was hard to change. But we could determine in advance which of the five or six had the strongest signal, and prime the phone to switch to that one. The baton would pass itself smoothly from hand to hand, and many fewer calls were dropped.

The development team

World's fair of communications

Thanks to the HiSilicon team's efficient R&D process, the solution was completed in no time. The next step was to verify whether the solution worked in a real-life environment. Did that mean carrying all the mobile phones and heavy equipment onto the train? No!

We first ran our solution through the virtual field-testing system mentioned earlier. When the results showed that the solution worked, it was time to roll out another secret weapon: the device and wireless joint testing lab.

The joint testing lab is a massive centre covering thousands of square metres. It costs over ¥100 million, and houses a lot of expensive equipment – each piece costing millions of yuan. The lab contains hundreds of real wireless base stations producing about 1,000 cells, simulating all of the different 2G, 3G and 4G services provided by major operators around the world. It can replicate real-life user environments such as offices, residential areas, high-speed railways, airports and sports stadiums. That is to say, we simulate all the real-life scenarios that major operators have to deal with. We call it the world's fair of communications.

A corner of the lab

The lab's results showed that the solution worked perfectly. However, Huawei's testing and verification process is more rigorous and complicated than that. The solution still had to go through one final test on a real high-speed train. So Mr Tang started his train travel again, taking HUAWEI Mate 10 series phones with him, as well as smartphones made by a number of other brands. For a week, he tested phones on the train, covering a total distance of about 40,000 km, almost equal to the circumference of the Earth. On all of his trips, there were only a few dropped calls in the gaps between network cells, and the Mate 10 outperformed all other phones. Not a single dropped call was caused by the phone itself.

When we were trying to address the signal issue for high-speed trains, the Mate 10 was still in the R&D process, so we were able to build the solution into Mate 10 phones. Since then, all Huawei phones have performed well on high-speed trains, but we have only fully solved the issue on the Beijing–Shanghai line. With an increasing number of people choosing high-speed trains as a major means of transportation, we have to extend the solution to more lines. And that work is still in process today.

The testing team

Huawei phones not only offer zero dropped calls on high-speed trains, they also boast other cutting-edge features. In 2017, the HUAWEI Mate 10 Pro achieved download speeds of 1.2 Gbps, the fastest network speed ever recorded on a phone. To achieve this, the phone, chipset and the wireless network must all be highly advanced and highly coordinated. Of course, 1.2 Gbps is achievable only in an ideal lab environment where phones and wireless networks are in prime condition. This super-fast experience is not yet available to consumers.

However, Huawei phones offer many benefits that phone users can experience in their everyday lives. For example, crisp call quality, fast internet speeds, instant network availability immediately upon plane landing, and split-second reaction times to grab those virtual red envelopes that we love to exchange during Chinese New Year. Under constant network conditions, Huawei phones always outperform those of other brands in these scenarios.

The Device Quality Report (2017, China Mobile) and Full-Frequency Device Communication Performance Assessment Report (2018, China Telecom) regarded our flagship phone, the HUAWEI Mate 10, as the best for communications. That made us incredibly proud and our hard work had been worth it.

I later bumped into the same passenger who had first complained to me about the poor signal on high-speed trains. He said that the signal on the Beijing–Shanghai line had improved significantly, and admired us for taking the initiative to resolve issues beyond our immediate responsibility. He also asked us how we did it. I answered him: "Communications is what Huawei does, and we are very good at it. We have fully developed phones, chipsets and wireless networks. Only Huawei can deliver the world's leading device–network–chipset synergy!"

Helping the Visually Impaired See the World

By Cui Qingyu

I have worked at Huawei for five years. I work in Huawei's consumer business, and I've seen the Emotion User Interface (EMUI) evolve from version 1.0 to 8.0. Performance has improved, user experience has improved, and I feel proud to have been part of it.

Over these years, we have achieved many firsts: the knuckle screenshot feature, simple desktop mode, Buddy Help and more. Every new version of EMUI brought us closer to our customers. But this time, our customers were the blind.

Our modest target: a feature for the visually impaired

"I am a visually impaired person. I hope that Huawei will provide accessible solutions so that members of the blind community in China can use Huawei phones too." This was an open letter signed by around a thousand customers in 2016, calling on Huawei to make information more accessible to those with disabilities. The letter was posted on the online forum – Huawei Club – and was taken very seriously by our handset planning department. It seemed that our phone operating systems had never considered the needs of people with disabilities before.

Looking at our own data samples and at many market surveys, we discovered that in China alone there are over 70 million people with reading and writing deficits. Some 92% of these people use Android phones. Several Chinese phone makers had made some efforts to serve disabled customers, but no phone maker had ever customized a phone for the blind.

If this group could be helped to operate Huawei phones with ease, it would be an important new feature in our EMUI. So we put together a list of blind users' biggest needs, and set ourselves a target for EMUI 5.1: include accessibility options and connect the blind to the world!

Finding and listening to authentic voices

To grow tall, a shoot must first emerge from the soil. But before this can happen, there are always unexpected problems to overcome.

We didn't have any experienced accessibility engineers among our staff, nor did we have any experience with accessibility testing or development. In fact, China didn't even have any accessibility standards. Would our designs for accessibility be accepted by the customers?

"Screen readers seem like far too much work. Every time you switch to a new menu, you have to listen for ages. Not very slick, is it?" said one user experience designer.

"But if we simplify it too much, users won't be able to understand," responded a member of the testing team.

We had three or four meetings to discuss the basic standards, but no one managed to convince the whole team. It was like we were blindfolded and feeling around in the dark for answers!

Since closed meetings weren't getting us the results we needed, we decided to look outward. We looked for experts in the field and real blind phone users. We soon became aware of the Information Accessibility Research Association, China's only non-governmental expert organization focusing on precisely these issues. After a few phone calls, we decided that we needed to meet up in person to see if their engineers could help us answer our questions.

When our four-person team arrived for the meeting, we were stunned. We walked into an office full of textured walkways, with many blind engineers hammering away at computers. They all had headphones on, and were using screen readers and other voice tools to listen as they typed in code at top speed. We were invited by the Association leaders to try out the interface for ourselves, but we found ourselves completely helpless in the darkness. The high-intensity stream of linguistic information just left our brains feeling battered. At that moment, we started to feel enormous respect for the visually impaired IT professionals around us. And we were determined to make the best phone functions we could for the visually impaired people out there.

No experience and no standards? We'll set the standard!

The engineers started to demonstrate the products that they had developed with one of their partners, and they told us very clearly the reasoning behind each feature in the design. I saw that there were some common features across all different products and platforms. Like sign language, these common features could serve as a shared basis for information accessibility in R&D, testing rules and any other area of work.

But putting this theory into practice immediately raised a thousand questions: "There's a constant deluge of information that needs transmission. Is voice fast enough?" and "You have to listen forever to complete one simple operation. Doesn't that make these phones too slow for modern life?"

These were the kinds of questions colleagues started asking as soon as the work started.

We brought our questions back to the Information Accessibility Research Association. A visually impaired IT smiled at us from his desk and said, "It's not that hard. Let's try them out." We simulated the process of getting on Taobao, the largest online shopping platform in China, and found that with the rapid-fire flow of speech through the screen reader, the blind engineer was no slower than a sighted person.

This showed us that the visually impaired develop a highly sensitive capacity to absorb and understand voice information. Fast and accurate streams of text are exactly what they need. However, we would have to continuously adjust the speed and complexity of these streams, and understand what is necessary for visually impaired users and what order of presentation best facilitates understanding. On this basis we could progressively improve the information-carrying stream and the accuracy of the reading.

By delving deeper into these questions over and over, we gradually developed Huawei's first standard for text-to-voice accessibility support. This standard would be an excellent basis for future product development.

Tips from a blind massage therapist

But is a standard enough? Would it be all smooth sailing from there? The standard was just the seed. To make it grow, there was a long process of cultivation to go through.

Building on the foundation of the accessibility standard, there was a whole project of development and adaptation to complete, covering the entire system and all applications. To support this, the Information Accessibility Research Association created a joint testing strategy that would apply their engineers' years of experience in accessibility systems to help us reliably and reproducibly test our systems as we iterated and developed them. We also found a group of 20-some people with visual impairments to serve as beta testers for us, so that we could hear their feedback first-hand.

During the development work, the feature managers and I would often go to massage clinics after work. In China, the massage industry traditionally hires a lot of visually impaired people. We asked the blind massage therapists about their experience using phones. This helped give us more insight into the experience of potential users.

"What is one function that you really wish our phones had?" we would ask.

The most important thing is a highly accurate input system. This is the most difficult thing for us to control, because the phone doesn't know the difference between words like "he," "she," and "it" (all of which are pronounced *ta* in Chinese, despite being written with different characters).

I can still remember the grimace on the face of the young blind man who explained this to me. After that massage, we went back and made the screen reader distinguish between the words "he," "she," and "it." When I returned to the same man, and showed him the screen reader reading out "masculine *ta*" (he), "feminine *ta*" (she), and "animal *ta*" (it), his face lit up.

Every time we talked to blind people, we came away with more inspiration. By experimenting over and over, we polished up each feature until it was absolutely clear how it ought to work.

We spent 3,600 hours on R&D, carried out 7,000 joint tests, and iterated our designs 200 times. Finally, we were able to produce an accessibility feature. Of course, just writing out the figures is simple, but each one of those hours brings memories of fierce concentration and commitment. I often think back on the day when we hit our targets, and the whole team burst into cheers and applause. The average age in our team was about 25, but these young adults jumped around like three-year-olds for the joy of seeing their project finally brought to life.

Over these years, we have achieved many firsts: the knuckle screenshot feature, simple desktop mode, Buddy Help and more.

The author Cui Qingyu

The proudest moment

In 2017, at the HUAWEI P10 launch event, EMUI 5.1 was unveiled with its new accessibility feature, called Talkback. It immediately won rave reviews in the media. Another blind massage therapist we know cheered the new feature, and told us, "This is great! I knew you guys could do it." That comment was the greatest reward we could wish to receive.

When I started working at Huawei in 2012, Android had not yet taken over the world. I had been involved in the development of the first EMUI, through the start of the HUAWEI P series, P1, and now I was seeing the opening up of our operating system with this accessibility project. Every idea along the way was generated by bringing people and ideas together. The process involved impassioned debate, going over each question time and again, and careful empirical research. There were moments when we thought about giving up. But we couldn't let our users down. We stayed committed to our original aspiration, *make it possible*. This mantra never failed to inspire us to greater energy and greater efforts.

Nothing makes you prouder than seeing the features you designed in use on a new Huawei phone, and serving hundreds of millions of users! Seeing that made me feel all my hours of hard work had not been wasted. And I'm sure that the next big success is not far away!

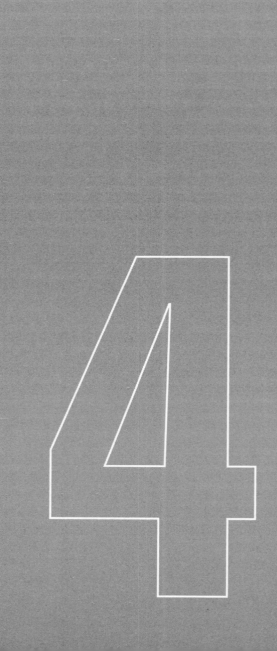

A Never-Ending Journey

Ending Journey

By He Gang

On 5 November 2011, while I was working in Japan on a wireless network expansion project, I got a call from Richard Yu asking me to work for him. The call came as a complete shock. But to my own surprise, I accepted the offer without any hesitation. Later, I realized that my quick acceptance may have been because this was what I wanted all along: creating smartphones global customers love.

Demanding quality products to deliver a quality experience

Huawei started producing phones in 2003 and had been making white label phones for operator brands. At the end of 2011, at a conference held in Sanya, Huawei decided that it should have its own brand and focus on making premium devices. So, Huawei started producing mid-range and high-end phones. At first, many in the industry, including many of our customers didn't understand why we were doing this. They didn't believe we could succeed.

To be sure, Huawei was going to be building its phone business up from nothing. I remember when I first transferred to the mobile phone department, I went to the Huaqiangbei Commercial Area in Shenzhen at the weekend. The Huaqiangbei Commercial Area is a barometer of China's consumer electronics market. By just looking around, you can see who the stronger players are. That day, I walked around the whole area, and was frustrated to see barely any Huawei logos on display, not to mention Huawei phones. But I knew that it was my responsibility to change this situation, so I was highly motivated to make a difference. I thought to myself, Huawei phones can definitely do better than this. We must change the current landscape.

Before I joined the Consumer BG, I worked on wireless network products. Over more than 20 years, with heavy investment in R&D and the most innovative and high-quality products and solutions, Huawei Wireless won the trust and support of its customers and earned the number one position in the wireless networks market. I believed that Huawei phones could do the same: deliver high-quality products and an inspired user experience by making the best innovations. At Huawei, we don't reduce costs by sacrificing user experience. Instead, we strive to improve the user experience, even when it means our costs must be a little higher. If we have US$10 and have to decide whether to invest these $10 in product R&D or marketing, we always choose the first option. This is in our genes. It's what the Huawei brand embodies.

Huawei is a company that is strong in execution. When we have an idea, we just roll up our sleeves and go full steam ahead to execute it. The first flagship smartphone we made was the HUAWEI P1. We positioned it as the world's thinnest smartphone to demonstrate our ambition. A lot of work had been done to make this phone: we used the thinnest display screen and designed a new battery and mobile phone architecture. Because it was so thin, there was no place for antennas. We tried many different solutions and finally decided to put antennas at the bottom of the phone. Unexpectedly, this gave the mobile phone a curvy look. As a result, this super-thin smartphone was well received by the market.

Our D series is targeted at business people, who demand higher performance. The D series were the first phones powered by quad-core processors. However, due to poor product positioning and understanding of target customers, the D1 and D2 were not very successful. After learning our lessons, we evolved the D series into the Mate series by focusing on the pain points of business people. We gave them large, 6-inch screens and mammoth 4,000 mAh batteries. The experience we gained making the Mate 1 and Mate 2 paved the way for the success of the Mate 7.

We met huge challenges when designing the Mate 7 in 2014. The Mate 7 was to be the world's first smartphone with a fingerprint sensor and an all-metal body. After considering performance, user experience, battery life, cooling and architecture, we estimated that 3,700 mAh was the maximum battery capacity we could use. This was smaller than the batteries in the Mate 1 and Mate 2. We couldn't afford to ruin our hard-won reputation for long battery life, so we told the R&D team to find a way to get a 4,000 mAh battery into the phone without sacrificing the industrial design or any other features. We put our very best design team on the problem, and managed to successfully expand the battery while keeping the industrial design and other key features. We got our large-capacity battery, fingerprint scanner, antennas, audio and heat dissipation all into a small package. The Mate 7 was well received by customers. The subsequent Mate 9 Pro, with a 5.5 inch organic light-emitting diode (OLED) curved screen, was also powered by a 4,000 mAh battery.

Competitive products are the key to success. Without competitive products, other efforts including the branding, marketing, sales channels and retail will be futile. We must also target a specific market segment, understand those people's needs, and address their biggest issues. Product planning must be completed at least a year in advance. Since consumer demands change over time, products can only be launched successfully to the market if they exceed the expectations of consumers one year in the future. It's like shooting at a moving target. Following product planning, we must have industry-leading R&D teams that help bring the product to life. Otherwise, we will always be uncertain whether a specific product can be successfully manufactured or not. To achieve sustained growth in Huawei's smartphone business, I made up my mind to build capabilities for every step in this end-to-end process. This was the only way to stop success from being a question of luck, and make it the inevitable result of good planning.

Building core capabilities
Adjusting organizational structure for better information sharing
To succeed, Huawei had to build core capabilities instead of relying solely on suppliers. We learned our lessons the hard way. When we first started developing phones, we were not able to convert many great ideas into a reality due to lack of core capabilities. We were limited by the capabilities of our partners, so we could not establish our own leading position.

How did we build core capabilities? Well, you can't cross the Pacific Ocean in a rowing boat. During the early years, Huawei's mobile phone R&D teams worked like a hundred little rowing boats. About a hundred products were developed every year and each product manager managed just a dozen or so R&D engineers. These teams worked independently or even competed with each other, and key components and software were not coordinated and consistent. Therefore, when we started producing smartphones, we didn't even keep the user interfaces consistent across different phones. It all added up to a poor user experience.

With the support of the company, we first cut our white label manufacturing to free up a large number of production resources, then allocated these resources to producing key products. At the same time, we adjusted the organizational structure to enable better sharing of resources. Collaboration is a more effective strategy than going it alone. We gradually brought the R&D forces of various departments together and began building specialist teams for product planning, industrial design, architecture design, multimedia, audio, communications, battery and software. Our capabilities started to develop bit by bit. At the same time, we focused resources on our core products to unleash the full potential of these resources.

For example, in order to deliver a consistent user experience, we put all of our software developers together in the Software Engineering Department and recruited a large number of managers and experts to develop our ability to create software. In 2014, we completely standardized the user interface with the release of EMUI 3.0. Later, we spent over a year focusing on eliminating any issues that were causing the software to lag or freeze. We managed to overcome numerous engineering difficulties, and made phones "fast off the shelf, fast always" by introducing artificial intelligence and deep learning technologies, designing an intelligent hardware resource management solution with HiSilicon, and boldly adopting an entirely new file system.

A camera is one of the key features for any modern phone. After our reorganization, we were able to lead the industry in developing a dual camera system that boosted the performance of our cameras. In order to take mobile photography to the next level, we reached out to the camera company Leica. After nearly one year of painstaking negotiation, we started working on lens technologies with Leica. Leica is a well-known ambassador of the high standards of German manufacturing. When we took Leica's high standards to some of the leading vendors in our industry, they were only able to get about 5% of the lenses rolling off their production lines to meet the standards.

But we all worked together, and gradually our vendor partners were able to improve their process yield up to 90%. At the same time, Huawei set up its own algorithm centre, which greatly enhanced colour performance. This combined approach of both joint and independent R&D helped Huawei to quickly build up core strengths in mobile photography and uncover the art of mobile photography.

Taking selfies with students

I expect everyone remembers the launch of the HUAWEI P20 series in Paris at the end of March 2018. The P20 Pro, powered by a high-capacity 4,000 mAh battery, featured an improved design with slim body and unique Morpho Aurora colour. It was also equipped with the world's first Leica Triple Camera. The professional image quality ranking site, DxOMark, gave the P20 Pro an overall score of 109, the highest ever for a mobile phone. It was rated by many tech media outlets as the best buy or the best smartphone of the year.

By adjusting our R&D organization, integrating resources and focusing on key technologies, we have built a team competent enough to challenge and compete with the world's leading phone makers. Our capabilities grew through a process of continuous competition, making us confident that we can continue to outperform our competitors.

Freedom to invest and sustain investment

Ever since the conference in Sanya, we have been continuously increasing our R&D spending in order to become an industry leader in development, testing, manufacturing, components and so on.

Today, Huawei has a super-large-scale automated testing lab. It can remotely control and test tens of thousands of mobile phones, allocating resources for different tests as required. With more than 30 years' experience in the communications industry and the technologies we have developed, we systematically test the communications performance of mobile phones in our lab, simulating the real-world routing and signals found on the networks of major global telecom operators.

The lab can carry out network-wide tests of high voice-traffic scenarios, simulating heavy network use 24/7 to identify potential issues. There are many separate testing modules, focused on network architecture, usage simulation, equipment ageing, displays, communications, battery life, sound quality and cameras. Each enables automatic testing and verification to ensure the quality and performance of Huawei phones.

In its early days, Huawei's consumer business was not very profitable. However, we realized that we shouldn't give up on investing in R&D on our own chips just to improve our short-term financial position. Without chips, we couldn't have core technologies, and would always be dependent on other companies. So we insisted on developing our own chips, including the K3V2 processor, which was widely criticized. I am eternally grateful for our customers' forgiveness and support. We were finally able to make Kirin chips a reality. This new chipset brought many of our ideas to life, such as adding security locks on chips, reducing energy consumption to support longer battery life and creating AI chips.

Today, we have R&D centres across the globe to address tough problems, such as the Aesthetics Research Centre in France, and centres of expertise in the US, Japan, Russia, Germany and Finland. At Huawei, experts from different countries work together to solve the problems users care about most. For example, the premium photography experience was made possible by experts from Finland, Japan, Russia and China. Our long-term strategy is to continue investing, and to make Huawei phones more competitive by constantly introducing new global talent and new cutting-edge technologies.

Stronger end-to-end capabilities

The mobile phone R&D team has a complete process, including product planning, software and hardware development, as well as customer insights, product delivery planning, production and supply, and sales support and services.

Customer insight is an in-depth analysis of customer needs, based on which different products are defined to meet the different needs of different groups. The success of the HUAWEI Mate series and P series was built on a deep understanding of customer needs. We found that the number of women buying Huawei phones was relatively low. Based on our market surveys and consumer intelligence, we created the sub-brand nova, targeting women and fashion-conscious young people, and delivering good-looking selfie phones they adore. Several nova phones have been launched, and have established nova's brand image as "good-looking selfie phones." We have also established a marketing support team that works with R&D during the product planning stage and explores the value a product can deliver in terms of the consumer experience and marketing. This helps to support global marketing activities and increase engagement with consumers.

Supply and delivery are key. Even if your product is well-planned and developed, if it is not readily shippable, all previous efforts will be in vain; it's like trying to scoop up water with a sieve. In the first few years, Huawei was trapped in a vicious circle: when a new device was launched, we didn't have enough stock ready to sell, and we scrambled to expedite the supply of materials. But when all the materials were finally available, we found our inventory piling up in the warehouse. We were also never able to launch a product to market simultaneously at home and outside China. Usually, products were launched outside China three to four months after the initial fanfare.

Now, thanks to sustained efforts to learn from our past experience, optimize product plans, and improve manufacturability and manufacturing efficiency, we have launched new products simultaneously across the globe. In the last two years, we have shipped over two million units per month for every newly released product.

In the past few years, we have launched the HUAWEI Mate series, P series, nova series, HUAWEI Enjoy series, Honor brand and other premium products. We increased our smartphone shipments from 20 million in 2011 to 153 million in 2017 by improving our planning and delivery capabilities. In 2018, we shipped more than 200 million phones.

Customer centricity and open collaboration for shared success

Staying customer-centric lies at the heart of everything we do

Huawei CEO Ren Zhengfei said, "The competitiveness of Huawei devices starts and ends with the consumer." The phone market changes fast and is highly competitive: consumers are demanding, new technologies continue to emerge and there is heavy reliance on channels and brand reputation. To succeed, we have to gain an in-depth understanding of consumers' explicit and implicit needs. We have to adopt the best possible technologies and solutions to satisfy and exceed consumers' expectations, and create a pleasant consumer experience throughout the journey, from nurturing to buying to servicing.

To keep the end-to-end user experience in mind, we developed a programme requiring managers and technical experts of certain grades to serve consumers in retail stores, spending some time every year working as sales promoters or service and maintenance engineers. To highlight the importance of after-sales services, we require each manager to handle at least one customer complaint every month. Our managers also have registered Weibo accounts so that they can interact with customers directly and hear their voices any time.

In 2014, we introduced the Net Promoter Score (NPS) model as part of our management of user experience, to help identify the issues users care about most. We also set up a Voice-of-the-Customer (VOC) system that puts all of our user feedback and suggestions onto one IT system. This can then guide our work and boost the quality-of-service indicators.

We have user survey teams and regional product centres to help us design smartphones that are more user-friendly, selfie teams to evaluate camera performance and optimize the photography experience, and dozens of other dedicated teams to ensure the best experiences (for example, split-second reaction times to grab virtual red envelopes at New Year, and a glitch-free call experience on high-speed trains). These teams continuously make incremental improvements in our phones so that we can always meet the rising expectations of our customers.

Shake hands with the world, and the world is in the palm of your hand
Today, a smartphone is used for more than just calling and texting.
It's also a camera, a music player, a radio and even a computer.
Though much smaller in size, a phone today can pack far more
computing power than computers from just a few years ago. As a
new player, we shouldn't close our doors and try to figure things
out on our own. We should make breakthrough innovations with
world-leading partners. This way, we will build a presence.

In addition to Leica, Huawei is also working with Porsche
Design and many other industry leaders. We aim to integrate the
essence of these industries into a single smartphone, in its appearance, crafting, materials, colour, sound, image and so forth. We
believe that embracing collaboration will help us grow rapidly. We
can deliver the best possible products and experience to consumers by using the best resources from across the globe.

Many people have asked me whether Huawei's success in
smartphones was a matter of luck or judgement. This is not an
easy question to answer. You may say our early success was mostly
a matter of luck. But today, every phone we launch is a winner, and
that can't just be luck.

Mr Ren says past performance is not a reliable indicator of
future success. No company can succeed all the time, including
Huawei. Huawei is committed to bringing digital to every person,
home and organization for a fully connected, intelligent world.
This is a never-ending journey. To go further, we must redouble
our efforts, listen to our customers with humility, and continue to
produce phones that global consumers love and trust.

Huawei smartphone shipments in 2018 topped 200 million units

From Luck to Skill:
The Story of the Mate Series

By Li Xiaolong

The Mate series is one of Huawei's more successful lines of phones. But not many people know the background: at the start, this series was mired in many setbacks and difficulties. A lot of people doubted the series would ever be a success. But we stuck to one principle: target the most pressing needs of our customers as precisely as we could. This principle was built into the DNA of the Mate series. We were sure that if we followed this principle, the Mate would be a success. All we needed was time and opportunity. And over the last five years, the Mate has been welcomed by consumers. Of course, there have been some challenges along the way, and I'd like to share some of those stories with you.

Huawei needs a flagship phone

This story is about the Mate, but I have to start with the P1. For Huawei, and for me, the P1 was the company's "Zero to One" moment. It was our first flagship smartphone under the Huawei brand. Before the P1, we had always produced phones in association with operators. Now we were building our own high-end brand name. This was a watershed in the history of Huawei.

In 2011, Huawei only sold low-end and mid-range phones, and we were still making feature phones. Richard Yu had just been appointed CEO of the Huawei Consumer BG, and he proposed that we build our own flagship smartphone. I had been in charge of feature phones, but my manager asked me to move from Xi'an to Shanghai to lead the development of our first flagship smartphone. As soon as I got off the plane in Shanghai, the first thing I did was to buy the flagship phones of other brands, so I could get an idea of what was on the market. At the time, my team and I had very limited experience with smartphones. The last smartphone I had bought for my own personal use had run the Windows Mobile operating system. Android was still a new platform at the time, and I knew nothing about it.

We quickly reached out to all the other Huawei teams who designed smartphones and learned what we could from them. Once we had a basic idea about how to build these products, we started to plan Huawei's first ever flagship smartphone, the P1. At the time, our thinking was simple: benchmark our phone against the phones that other suppliers already had on the market, use leading technology for each function, and give our customers the best possible experience in every area. So, we selected the very best solutions for the phone's form factor, processor, operating system, memory, camera, interior components and battery. In terms of the structural design, we packed the most advanced components as closely as possible. The P1 had more new components than any other Huawei phone at that time, and it was much harder to develop than we had imagined. By the time the P1 hit the shelves, it was considerably over budget.

In 2012, we finally launched the P1 onto the market, with great expectations. It was the first ever Chinese phone to be produced with industry-leading quality. Unfortunately, the market's response was a slap in the face. Our global sales were only a few hundred thousand units, nowhere near what leading phone brands achieved, and significantly worse than the sales of Huawei's own low-end and mid-range phones.

From hope to hopeless … We were left consoling ourselves with poor excuses: "It was just our first attempt … At least we tested the waters …" But we had to look back at what had really gone wrong. When you make a phone, you cannot just pursue high performance. Just putting all of the most advanced technologies into one phone is no guarantee of success. You need expertise in a whole range of other areas. For example, branding: we set the price of the P1 at ¥2,999, making it the most expensive Chinese-made phone on the market. But our customers still thought of Huawei phones as freebies that their broadband providers handed out when they signed a contract. Most people simply weren't ready to pay that much for a Huawei phone.

Another example: retail expertise. The P1 was one of our first forays into the retail market. We had previously only sold directly to corporate customers. Most retailers had little interest in working with us, because our brand was not attractive at that time. Today, you can see the Huawei logo everywhere, but that was not the case back then. We never managed to get the P1 shelf space in either Gome or Suning, China's two biggest electronics retail chains. In 2012, the Consumer BG started mobilizing employees to go out and personally promote Huawei phones in stores.

I found that the stores I was assigned to didn't even sell the P1. It was a humbling moment.

Despite the problems, we had learned many lessons from this process. Huawei's flagship smartphones had set sail, and everyone kept their eyes on the future and the successes to come.

A product to keep us going

Those successes took longer than any of us had imagined. For close to a year, we launched a series of high-end phones and were met with crushing defeat. It seemed like the harder we tried, the worse we did. The team was in trouble, and morale sank through the floor. "Why can't we get this right?" we kept wondering, as the frustration continued. It was also hitting us personally. So long as our phones were losing money, there was nothing in the bonus pot for my team.

We needed a product that could sustain our operations. With these revised expectations in mind, we started the development of the Mate 1. The trend at that time was for screens to get fractionally bigger each year. We thought, can't we just skip to the end of this process? Design a phone that has the largest possible screen, while staying small enough to hold in the hand? The other big issue with smartphones was battery life. There were no phones with massive screens and super-long charge cycles, so we focused on those two issues. We planned to make a 6.1-inch screen, which would be our unique selling point. For the other functions and specifications, all we wanted was to make sure they didn't let our customers down. We'd go with tried-and-tested components, and minimize our costs.

When the product rolled off the production line, both the online and offline sales teams wanted to sell it, because the big screen was a great selling point. It gave them something to work with. However, both teams were also somewhat hesitant, because none of our previous phones had sold well. With no one quite ready to commit, management made the decision: we would make two different editions, with different amounts of memory; and they would be sold by both teams. Unfortunately, coordination between the teams was not easy. One team wanted one tagline, the other team preferred another slogan, and it took a lot of meetings to get everyone on the same page. During the process, we made some mistakes in our stock projections. So when sales took off, we didn't have enough units in stock. By the time we had stocked up, the phone had stopped selling.

Huawei phones only sold in small numbers back then, so even though the first Mate phone did not sell a huge number of units, for us, it was a success. Unfortunately, we had a lot of excess materials (mainly the batteries and screens, because of their long lead times), and that waste devoured all of our profits and then some.

We had warehouses full of screens and batteries. We had to find a way to use them up. So, the development of the Mate 2 was really forced upon us. Our selling point would once again be the big screen, but this time we fitted the phone with Huawei's first-generation system-on-a-chip, the Kirin 910. It was designed for 4G networks, and it was ahead of any other chip the industry had to offer. But the Mate 2 was not attractive enough as a whole package, and as before sales were lukewarm. With two generations under its belt, the Mate series was just about staying out of the red, but hadn't delivered any real profits.

What we didn't realize at the time was that these two Mate phones, with moderate sales, had paved the way for our future success. Smartphones universally suffered from short battery lives, and the Mate 1 and Mate 2 had managed to combine a large screen with a long-lasting battery. Customers loved it, and we were starting to build a following of Mate fans. These fans had a very distinctive user profile, and their needs helped us set our direction as we developed the Mate 7, which was destined to be our breakout product.

The Mate series is
one of Huawei's more
successful lines of
phones. But not many
people know the
background: at the
start, this series was
mired in many setbacks
and difficulties.

Here's one for the fans ...

At one of our meetings in 2013, an industrial designer showed us a new design for a phone that made me very excited. It was an all-metal body with a huge screen, and it looked both elegant and understated. I said to myself, "This is the product that I want." This became the prototype design for the Mate 7, from which we planned the next Mate phone.

As I mentioned above, the Mate 1 and Mate 2 may not have been financial blockbusters, but they did give us a much more valuable asset: a group of committed Mate fans. Our customer surveys gave us a clear picture of these consumers. They were often elite professionals, with a measured level of success; they had some experience of the good life; and their careers were on the up and up. But they had many responsibilities – children, elderly parents, mortgages, car loans etc.

What did they want from a mobile phone? They used their phones for work as well as for leisure, so they preferred a bigger screen. They were heavy users, so battery life was extremely important. They liked the Mate because of the large screen and the long-lasting battery, so it was vital to keep these two strengths. Their phones were necessary tools for their work, so high performance was essential. The large screen meant that we would need a compact design, with a high screen-to-body ratio, and it would need to look solid and serious to suit a person of status and importance.

With this, the project to build the next phone, codenamed Jazz, began. A big screen and a powerful battery were already strengths of the Mate series. To achieve the high performance that we wanted, we decided to use Huawei's latest Kirin chip at the time, the 920. This was the first time our processors would have a real edge over the competition. To maintain smaller dimensions, we racked our brains for ways to pack the components together. At one point, we even considered putting the camera at the bottom of the phone, to shave 2 mm off the length. But if we had gone through with it, our phone users would have been shooting selfies from underneath their chins, and would have squashed faces in every picture. This was hardly the experience we wanted our users to have, so we dropped this idea.

We also added a completely new function with a fingerprint scanner that could unlock the phone. Today, this is nothing major, but five years ago this function did not exist on any phone on the market, and there were no fingerprint chipsets available off the shelf. Back then, the iPhone 5s had not yet been launched, and other phones with fingerprint scanners first required a button-press, then a swipe. The inclusion of this new function was one of our biggest internal controversies: "It's a white elephant! It's expensive, and it bulks up the phone for no added value!" and "It's so practical! This function is going to send the phone flying off the shelves!"

The row went on and on. I supported the fingerprint function. I talked about this situation: imagine you've been working all day, you're tired and you want to call your family – your parents, or your wife and children. The last thing you want to do is enter a password to unlock your phone.

A little story like this is not a magic spell. It didn't persuade everyone straight away. But we did in the end decide to include the fingerprint function – a decision which led directly to the next controversy: whether we put it on the front or the back of the phone. I was adamant that the scanner should go on the back of the phone, because in a phone with a big screen, the form factor is crucial. A fingerprint scanner could be embedded into the back of the phone without increasing the dimensions, and it would also be the right place for our customers. In the end, the market proved that this was the right decision. The rear-mounted fingerprint scanner became one of the phone's most celebrated features.

Of course, the Mate 7 was not a perfect phone. Considerations of cost meant that we were unable to use the very best components for every part. We listed out the cost of the phone item by item, and were uncompromising in what we decided to eliminate. Every time we removed something it hurt, but it was necessary. In the end, we couldn't spend much on the camera. At the time we didn't think our customers would be that interested in the camera function.

So, function by function and feature by feature, we finalized the design and the specifications of the phone. Unlike the first two Mate phones, we had complete clarity on what we wanted to achieve with this product. We had to respond to each one of the needs of our target consumers, and in the end we were fully confident in our product.

When we got together to decide the marketing strategy, a lot of people said that it would be a mistake to call this phone the Mate 3. Neither the Mate 1 nor Mate 2 had sold well, so the wholesalers and retailers were not particularly confident in the Mate series. Continuing with the Mate name might lead to poor sales. There was a proposal to call this the D series, and another to call it the X. By the end of the meeting it was decided that the phone would be called the D7. It looked like the end of the Mate line, but after the meeting I went and lobbied the executives to keep the name. My reason was simple: Mate is a friend, and this was a phone you could rely on. You didn't have to worry about its battery running down, or about the system glitching. You could feel relaxed, because this was your loyal friend. After we had talked it through, we gave the phone the name Mate 7. It's an interesting thing to look back on, that the Mate series was very nearly "two strikes and you're out."

In 2014, after a dangerous birth, the Mate 7 was launched for sale.

Launch of the HUAWEI Mate 7 in Berlin

A well-planned, but unexpected, blockbuster

"Xiaolong, how many units do you think the Mate 7 is going to ship?" a colleague from another team asked me, soon before the phone hit the shelves.

"1.2 million," I claimed. To be honest, I was stretching. If we could sell 800,000 to 900,000 units, it would have been a big win for us. In terms of technology, the Mate 7 was a cutting-edge phone. And in order to sell a lot of phones, you need a top-quality product. But we had experienced too many failures to think that this was enough.

At the launch event, we announced the price of ¥2,999 for the standard edition and ¥3,699 for the premium edition, which was received by a shocked silence. No Chinese-made phone had ever sold for more than ¥3,000, and a lot of people thought we had made the wrong choice. They said the Huawei brand could not support a phone costing more than ¥3,000. This phone, they said, was just going to be another Mate failure.

With four months left to go in 2014, our China regional office held a meeting in Shanghai, and asked sales teams from different parts of the country how many Mate 7 phones they thought they would sell in the next four months. The leader of the representative office with the most sales in China came up onto the stage and said: "10,000." My heart sank. If our biggest sales team only wanted to take such a small shipment, they must not have seen any prospects for this product. To make things worse, other teams in the hall started calling out, "10,000? You must be joking! There's no way you'll move that many."

I also saw a blog post written by an engineer who worked on Vmall, Huawei's online store, which said they were worried about too many people logging on to buy the phone and overwhelming the servers. However, when he saw the price of the Mate 7, he felt a weight was lifted from his shoulders, because at that price, there was little chance of too much traffic.

Amid all of these negative signs, I went back and reviewed our original strategy once more. First, the product did not need to be cutting edge in every way, but it had to be high quality, with some clear selling points. Second, the phone was targeted precisely at the pain points of our target customer group, and these customers were powerful brand advocates who would promote us through word-of-mouth. Third, the product and the brand needed to be well-matched, but it was OK to be a little aspirational, and our positioning was still reasonable. We hadn't tried to pose as something we couldn't justify. Fourth, with a few years' experience under our belt, Huawei's ability to sell phones was improving. We had transformed ourselves in terms of marketing, sales channels and retail capabilities.

We had run through these factors forward and back, over and again, and we had cut the initial production run down to three months' inventory. If we did start to sell well, we could gear up production. And if sales were lower than predicted, we wouldn't be left with a massive backlog of stock. All that was left was to wait and see what would happen.

Just one week after the Mate 7 hit the shelves, we started to receive messages from across China: "The Mate 7 has sold out, send more stock." The engineer who wrote the blog post about traffic volume on the online store wrote a follow-up blog, saying that the number of buyers on the store for the Mate 7 were rising every day, and it was starting to worry him. He was frantically adding capacity to make sure the servers didn't get paralysed by the traffic.

Two weeks after the launch, you couldn't get a Mate 7 for asking. All the retailers who previously didn't want to work with Huawei were now clamouring to be our partners. They were setting up special Huawei islands in their stores and putting the Huawei logo above their doors. Many stores that sold phones were putting up blackboards outside with "Mate 7 in stock" on them just to get people into the store. Our team members were suddenly finding themselves to be very socially desirable, with old friends and acquaintances rekindling relationships to ask, "Is there any chance you can help me get a Mate 7?"

The HUAWEI Mate 7 was named new smartphone of the year 2015 by Hurun, publisher of China's rich list

Sales of the Mate 7 blew everyone's projections out of the water, including those by me and my team. This was a huge and sorely needed confidence booster for us, and the sales figures also brought us new kinds of experience and expertise in branding, marketing, sales channel management and retailing.

Expanding our appeal

The Mate 7 was a hit, and now we were able to invest more resources in the Mate series. The big screen, long-lasting battery, high performance, compact design – all of these were now firmly established as part of the DNA of a Mate phone. From the Mate 8 to the Mate 10, we followed the same pattern. We upgraded the processors, appearance, cameras and screens, so that in each iteration we were using the very best technologies available at that time, bringing the best experience to our customers. We let our costs rise so that we could give customers the very best product. Our image improved, allowing us to position the phone as more of a premium product. Our brand grew stronger, and was able to support higher prices, helping us develop more competitive phones that deliver better experiences. This created a virtuous cycle of improvement.

In particular, I want to mention the Mate 9 Pro, which had the smallest screen of any Mate phone, at just 5.5 inches. Many people asked why we would abandon the large screen. Wasn't it a key selling point of the Mate? But we weren't just giving up on our unique selling point. Our goal was to give more people the chance to experience the inspired performance of Huawei phones.

You have to think about it in terms of the customer habits. For every phone maker in the world, except Huawei, small-screen phones outsell big-screen phones. In fact, large-screen phones can be seen as a niche market. The consumer mainstream is the smaller screen. For example, in China, many female consumers find the Mate to be too big, and it doesn't fit comfortably in their hand. Mate phones have never sold very well in Western Europe, and one of the major reasons is that Europeans find the Mate screen too big. It's not what they are used to in a smartphone.

Therefore, I always had a vision of extending the reach of the Mate, and bringing the Mate experience to more users. When we were planning the Mate 9, I suggested developing the Mate 9 Pro, with a 5.5-inch screen that matched the standard size. In every other respect, it would be identical to the Mate 9: a top-of-the-range phone.

The difference between 5.9 and 5.5 inches may not sound like much, but in the world of the smartphone, where every millimetre counts, shrinking the body by 0.4 inches makes the phone much more difficult to design. To give you the simplest example, when the phone was shrunk down, the Mate 9's 4,000 mAh battery no longer fit in the case, and there was a danger that the battery life would be affected. We demanded that the Mate 9 Pro achieve the smaller dimensions without impacting the specifications at all. If we couldn't give our consumers an inspired experience and a world-beating product, then we might as well give them nothing at all. So, our battery team got down to work, and slowly, painstakingly, raised the capacity of the smaller battery from 3,700 mAh to 4,000 mAh.

As the design became more challenging, the cost went up. To fit the same components into a smaller space, the Mate 9 Pro had to use a more expensive OLED screen. The Huawei Consumer management wanted to cancel the phone on several occasions because the cost was too high, and they thought we couldn't offer it to our customers for a reasonable price. But I stuck to my guns. I wanted the Mate 9 Pro to take us to a larger and richer group of consumers. I was willing to sacrifice some profits and accept slimmer margins. At one meeting, I joked, "We want the Mate 9 Pro to be a phone that might lose customers because of the price, but will never lose a customer because of its quality."

The retail price for the Mate 9 Pro was finally set at 4,699 yuan for the standard edition and 5,299 yuan for the premium edition. Personally, I don't think the value of that phone was in the money it made for us, but in the statement it made. The phone had a smaller screen, but with big-screen performance and battery life. This showed the world the strength of our R&D, and it raised our brand to another level, bringing more high-end consumers into contact with Huawei. The phone also let everyone know that the Huawei brand is a brand that can support top-end phones. Our customer surveys showed that the Mate Pro did indeed attract the largest number of high-value consumers.

From the first generation of the Mate in 2013 to the Mate 10, the series has a history of just five years. But in that time, we put out ten phones in six generations. Some of them have been hits, and some of them have underperformed. Many complex factors can affect the success of a single phone. Sales are always a combination of skill and luck, and this is something we are still working out ourselves. But when I look at the entire Mate series, I can proudly say that the bit of success we have achieved today was the result of good work by our team. No matter how many times we stumbled, we always got back on our feet, and kept our eyes fixed on the ultimate goal: look, that is where our customers are.

Dancing on the Head of a Pin

By Cai Xiaogen

Here in the Huawei Device Manufacturing Department, our job as engineers is to develop the manufacturing technologies that produce the beautiful phones our designers imagine, at scale and to consistently high standards. As phone screens get bigger and bigger, it's becoming more difficult to securely attach them to a phone frame. How can we keep the structure of the phones solid? Answering questions like this is our job.

1.5 mm is all we need

In July 2011, I was still fairly new to Huawei. One day, my manager Mr Kang suddenly told me, "You're going to be in charge of the new product introduction process for the HXX1."[1]

New product introduction (NPI) means taking charge of the entire verification process for a new product, from the first proto-typing to full-scale production. It is an important step in ensuring the smooth and high-quality delivery of products. HXX1 was the new flagship phone we were developing at the time. It was a key part of Huawei's market strategy, and I was very proud to take part in the design of something so important. That was the beginning of my long journey in the world of screens and attaching them to phone frames.

The industrial design – the initial design specification for the physical shape of the product – reduced the width of the contact surface around the screen, where the screen is attached to the phone body, from 2.5 mm to 1.5 mm. This was necessary for better viewing experience, but was also a big challenge. It made the touchscreen easily detach from the frame as screen adhesives were an area in which Huawei lagged behind our competitors. We had never made a phone with such a narrow adhesive area before.

What is this contact surface? In simple terms, a phone is essentially a frame with a touchscreen resting on top. We use double-sided adhesive tape to attach the touchscreen securely, so that it doesn't fall off the phone. The width of the strip where the screen and the frame touch is a key factor in how easy it is to secure the screen.

We started with the test production of the new phone, and took the test models for reliability testing. This process assesses whether the phone will work properly throughout its life. For example, we drop the phone from a certain height and at certain angles, and we toss it around in a tumbler drum of a certain size. If the phone passes these reliability tests, it can be sold in stores. The wait for the reliability testing results is always a very nerve-racking time. Every minute seems like an hour.

When we finally got our hands on the test results for the HXX1, they were a massive shock. One out of every ten phones was found to have its screen detached from its phone frame. That was 100 times higher than the 0.1% defect rate allowed for this kind of test. It meant that in every 100 phones, ten phones would need repairs, directly increasing our costs by 10%. The mobile phone industry operates on thin margins. A 10% increase in costs would mean that we would have to cancel the launch of this product, and all of the R&D work that had been done to date would be wasted. This could deal a fatal blow to Huawei as a phone vendor.

Everyone dived into fixing the problem. We focused hard, and for three full months we lived and breathed phone engineering. We analysed every angle, filling whiteboards with potential problem factors, test results and verification practices. We filled a thick notebook with test data alone. We finally finished tracking down all of the factors that would cause the screen to detach from the phone frame, and made the corresponding crucial changes to our process: a smoother finish on the phone body, more precision in the application of the tape, and more pressure when we fixed the screen to the body. With these changes, our defect rate fell from 10% to an acceptable 0.1%, and finally we were able to pass the reliability tests. Everyone let out a sigh of relief, and as the man in charge of manufacturing technology I was especially relieved. Finally, my first product could progress to full-scale production!

Specifications for double-sided tape

We had solved the problem for HXX1, but the screen-to-body ratio continued to grow, and the width of the contact surface was getting narrower and narrower. As a result, the problem of securing touchscreens to phone frames arose again and again in other

Huawei products. Our product lines were constantly putting out fires and redoing their work. Our R&D and delivery teams were spending all their time responding to problems – patching a problem here, then rushing away to deal with another one on another product, over and over.

Finally, Wang, who was the head of design engineering, called everyone together and told us that we needed a comprehensive solution to this issue. We had to work out proper process specifications for a good bond between screen and body.

She was right: constantly putting out fires was no way to work. We needed to get ahead of the problem, so that we could be certain of guaranteed quality every time.

We set up a dedicated project team, led by Luo, who worked in product design engineering. I was on the project team, too. The first thing we had to do was to work out how double-sided tape, touchscreens and the frame interacted. We spent our days in the lab testing exactly what kind of bonds the tape would make between screen and frame under what conditions. There were 15 different types of adhesive tape in common use across the industry, and more than 30 different tests that were used to measure the quality of the adhesive bond. We ran each test three to five times, and from the resulting nearly 100 datasets, we worked out how these different types of tape compared to one another. Finally, we selected three types of tape that met our needs, and developed minimum design specifications that would ensure a firm bond between touchscreen and frame.

We also went to check all of the products that were in the design, trial production or full-scale production phase. We corrected any products that failed to meet the design, materials control and quality process standards we had developed. To make sure that all of these changes were being put into practice, we visited five EMS (electronics manufacturing services) providers and six suppliers in two weeks, and went through a checklist of several dozen items with them, one by one. We developed a set of more than 20 control requirements for product design, materials and quality, and checked with a dozen experts from different domains at Huawei, so that we could ensure that all the design issues were perfectly resolved for every single product.

In the six months we spent working on this project, we developed all of the process specifications required, and ensured that these specifications were strictly implemented. All of this hard work paid off. In the 2013 quality report, the fault feedback ratio (FFR) for all phones had fallen to less than 0.03%. The specification laid the groundwork for the bonding between touchscreens and phone frame. In a way, we were pioneers, providing a solid foundation on which many future products would be built.

Trucking along a road 0.8 mm wide

In 2013, screens continued to grow, with the screen-to-body ratio pushing for maximum. Phone makers around the world were racking their brains to develop a better industrial design, and once again we all faced the challenge of screen adhesion. This time, the contact surface width narrowed from 1.5 mm to less than 0.8 mm. This time, there was no way that the tape currently available would do what Huawei needed them to do. We would have to use a method that Huawei had never tried before: glue.

Gluing a phone screen was a rather different process from the kind of gluing that you might be familiar with. We had to apply the glue in milligram quantities to a surface just 0.8 mm wide. It was like driving a truck along a mountain road exactly 2.2 metres wide. An inch to the right, and down you plunge; an inch to the left, and you crash into the cliff.

How were we to apply the glue accurately to this 0.8 mm surface? Our production line turned out phones at a rate of 2,000 to 3,000 every day. We only had a 10 mg margin of error when applying the glue on each device. What kind of equipment could achieve that precision? How were we to manage the people operating the machinery, to ensure consistent quality? We had no answers to these questions.

After much discussion and consideration of factors including manufacturability, stability and process feasibility, we decided that we needed specialist equipment. We had no experience buying this kind of equipment, so we would first have to research exactly what functions it needed. After nearly two months of research, we were finally able to confirm two equipment vendors and put their equipment on the line for testing.

The equipment was installed, but on the first day our defect rate sat at an unacceptable 20%. The main reason was excess adhesive, glue seeping out onto the exterior of the phone. We needed to scrape the glue and polish the defective phones using a 0.1 mm thin sheet and dust-free cloth. Clearing one defective unit took five to ten minutes, but each day there were nearly 200 defective phones. This would cause a massive increase in our workload, and our staff complained bitterly.

So what was the cause of the problem? We took the 200 defective phones, and broke them down into six categories of problems, including issues like glue on the screen, glue not applied to the contact surface, and gaps in the glue. Then we were able to identify the cause of each problem, adjust the glue dispensers, and check that the new settings had solved the problem and had not caused any new problems in turn. Once the six adjustments had been made, we used the data collected in the verification process to analyse the machine's performance, and developed a final specification for the glue dispensers.

To make sure we had really solved the problems, the project team borrowed another 100 phone frames, applied the glue and attached the touchscreen. This time we got a defect rate of 2%, which was a huge relief; 2% was still much higher than our goal of 0.5%, but at least we were moving in the right direction. When we finally got that 2% result, everyone suddenly noticed that it was already the middle of the night. We headed out to a local roadside diner that we liked, and the owner fired up the wok for us. The joy of having made progress on our challenge made that meal one of the best I've ever tasted.

Over the next week, we continued to refine the parameters of our glue dispenser, and finally drove the defect rate down to less than 0.3%. That was within the desired range. The phones went into full-scale production, and the glue equipment on the production lines worked perfectly. Now everyone knew what the new process specifications were. We also worked with R&D to develop an explicit set of specifications for the glue dispensing process, and that gave us a good base for all future gluing process issues.

At Huawei,
progress never stops.

Trucking along a road four hairs wide

Now that we knew how to glue screens, we started using the gluing process on many more phones. Inevitably, that meant an increasingly higher bar. In 2015, our contact surface shrank again, down to 0.4 mm. This was just half of what we had to work with previously, and only the width of four human hairs laid side by side. This really was like dancing on the head of a pin, with zero room for error. If 0.8 mm felt like driving a truck down a mountain road, then 0.4 mm felt like trying to fly a jumbo jet along it!

Cai, the manufacturing liaison, led the team. Luo and Min took responsibility for NPI, and the manufacturing process was managed by Jing and Sun. To achieve the precision we needed, we had to get creative, and the team really rose to the occasion. Working with R&D, we filled whiteboards with every possible factor that could get in the way of our goal – and several impossible factors, too! We analysed each one, talked over the results, and worked out how we could handle them. It sounds simple enough, but this work was incredibly tedious.

Once we had the ideas worked out, we had to verify everything. Unfortunately, the verification tests showed that some touchscreens were detaching from the phone frame.

In order to see what was going wrong, we needed to get inside the defective products, but the only way to do that was to literally grind them until we could see the cross-section that we needed. So out came the grinding wheel, and we got to work. It took 30 minutes to an hour to grind out one cross-section of a phone, and for each defective unit, we might have to look at ten different sections, each of which would require multiple different measurements. It was an extremely time-consuming procedure. But after grinding open about ten different units, we found the answer. The problem was with the contact surface on edge of the phone frame. As I said, the 0.4 mm width made it like flying a plane down a mountain road. We could actually get the plane on the road, but when the road went into switchbacks, there was no way to get the plane around the corners without skidding off the track. The road needed to be straight. All of this made us remember once again how the devil really is in the details.

Over the next four months, every defect that involved a separation of touchscreen from phone frame was a torment for our team. Every time, the root cause was some tiny detail – but in each case, the tiny detail was also very important. For example, one time it was because a micrometre-thick layer of optical adhesive had been left on the surface of the screen. This layer could only be seen under a microscope at 20× magnification, but even these tiny imperfections were enough to interfere with the bonding process, and cause the phone to fail its reliability tests. Each of these problems helped us improve our ability to deal with a 0.4 mm contact surface a little more. The learning process was painful, but, in the end, the results were impressive.

Let no one put them asunder

At Huawei, progress never stops. Even as we improved our ability to control screen adhesion on a narrow contact surface, we realized that the use of glue rather than tape had lengthened the production process by 24 hours. When the screens were first attached, they had to be held under pressure for two hours to bond properly to the phone frame, and for the next 22 hours they could not be moved. So, a process that used to take three days now took four days to complete. That meant more time storing materials, and more pressure on our warehouses, raising costs for the production process as a whole. At this point the project team set a new target: halve the production time!

Mr Ye, our manager, said, "This is going to shorten our delivery time, make us more competitive and cut the cost of the fixture equipment. We must succeed."

We were going to have to refine our processes even further.

In early 2017, Manufacturing welcomed a team leader, the materials specialist Dr Qu. We decided to focus first on running verification tests to obtain good data, then on cutting the drying time for the glue down to ten hours. Dr Qu visited 2012 Labs at least once a week to talk to the product design engineering experts there. They examined the bond formed when different materials were used, when the bond was left to set for 6 hours, 8 hours, 10 hours and 22 hours, different humidity and the impact of glue creep.

In all, over 30 sets of parameters were tested. Once the data had been collected on these 30 experiments, we were able to demonstrate that a ten-hour curing period was functionally the same as a 22-hour period. A two-plus-ten-hour process was sufficient for us to pass our reliability tests, so this became our standard timing going forward.

This change put us out ahead of the rest of the industry. We can now proudly state that the glue dispensing technology used by Huawei Device Manufacturing is the standard to which everyone else aspires. And we have not stopped improving. We continue to explore the most cutting-edge process technologies to find ways to attach our touchscreens to phone frames even more securely.

A photograph to celebrate the success of the 0.4 mm solution
(author, Cai Xiaogen, centre)

A few days ago, a colleague said to me, "Just think – all those years, all those people, and all of that effort, just for the sake of sticking a screen to a phone frame!"

That's right. Ever since I started at this company, I have focused on just one thing: sticking touchscreens to phone frames securely. I have seen generations of technology come and go, from double-sided tape to glue, from 1.5 mm contact surfaces to just 0.4 mm. Five years of hard work, five years of learning ever-more-complex technologies, and the goal that has driven me all this time: once phone frame and touchscreen have been joined together, let no one put them asunder!

1   HXX1 is not an actual product name.

Twinkle, Twinkle, Twinkle, Little Star

By Nie Xingxing

"Young people should put themselves out there and commit to something."

That was what my adviser said to me when I was just finishing up my master's degree. I wrote it down in my diary on 17 February 2014. That day, I officially walked out of my university for the very last time, and entered the Software Development Department in the Consumer BG at Huawei's Beijing Research Centre. It was the first day of my career, and the beginning of an amazing journey.

A hatchling takes wing

When I first started, I was assigned to the log system development team – known in-house as "the sparrows." It was only a small team, but our job was to collect logs for all of the R&D teams working on phones and tablets. The log system is responsible for collecting error messages every time something goes wrong with a phone. These logs are vital for diagnosing problems and helping us provide the best possible customer experience.

When I joined the team, it was just about to start working on version 5.0 of the log system. There were a lot of problems to be solved, and a lot of development to do. As the newest hatchling among the sparrows, I was keen to take on a challenge and prove myself.

However, my university courses had barely touched on phone testing software. For the first few days of my new job, I was just staring at a stack of files that I couldn't understand at all. I didn't know where to start, so all I could do was watch what my colleagues were doing. My anxiety levels skyrocketed. I kept thinking to myself, "Don't fail before you've even started!"

In that first week, I devoured the basics of the Android system, the files involved, the code and the architecture for specific operations. I gulped down everything the team had learned in three years.

One morning during my second week, I strode over to the workstation where my mentor sat.

"I'm ready," I told him. "What do you have for me to do?"

My mentor looked at me and said, "Come and work on the log system's memory alerts."

This function displays pop-up messages reminding users how much memory their log files are taking up, to help them make sure enough memory is available. It didn't seem like a big job, so I immediately dived in: I started coding away, and, in just one day, I had completed all of the coding required. In fact, I was feeling quite pleased with myself.

Shortly before the end of day, I took a demo over to my mentor, expecting some hearty congratulations. But when my mentor plugged it into the system and tested it, a fault popped up: "System error."

I was stunned. It was a major blow to my confidence, and I could feel my face turning red. I couldn't even look at my mentor. What was the problem? It turned out that when I was coding, I forgot to thoroughly analyse the supporting architecture in these mobile devices. I didn't think about what would happen when a phone's memory was full, or when the log files were exceptionally big. And I hadn't tested the code myself before showing my mentor.

"R&D is a process that starts with design, and ends with verification," he explained patiently. "Being a good developer means polishing your skills in design, coding and testing. Don't rush into the coding, forgetting the initial design and final testing. Everything we do has to serve our colleagues whose work will depend on ours. And ultimately it has to serve consumers."

This is one of the most important lessons I've learned at Huawei: before you launch a rocket, you have to be sure that you have a solid base to blast off from. So, the next day, I buckled down and considered the problem I was trying to solve, analysed the design requirements and thought about what sort of situations might arise when customers used the phone. Within a week, I had completed my solution design, coding and testing. This time when I delivered my 400 lines of code, it passed verification testing on the first try.

I learned a huge amount
from this experience.
At first I needed someone
to hold my hand, but, soon
enough, this little sparrow
had learned to fly.

The author, Nie Xingxing

Completing my first job helped me win some of my confidence back, and, from that point on, I threw myself into dealing with protocol logs, log management, log tools, architectural refactoring and so on. Now I was managing to perform each task at a high level.

When we were working on version 5.1, I was appointed as our team's ambassador. Over the course of a month, I visited lots of different research centres, encouraging the teams to incorporate our "service radar" into ten of their core services. I surveyed more than 100 system exceptions to help us quickly determine what we needed to focus on. This meant that before the product ever reached our consumers, we had helped all the different R&D teams identify many potential problems.

I learned a huge amount from this experience. At first I needed someone to hold my hand, but soon enough, this little sparrow had learned to fly.

Our consumers deserve the stars and the moon

Now that I had finished a few projects, my technical skills were developing nicely. In March 2016, the department head told me, "Our department is going to be taking on a new project. We are going to develop an intelligent global search function. It will be your job to lead a five-person team to take it on."

This was the first time I had my own team, and a brand new project. I was excited, but also a little worried. I'd only been at the company for two years, and now I was already leading my own team. I wasn't sure I'd be able to pull it off. But Huawei is a company that likes to give young people a chance. My manager encouraged me, and the fact that I had already been part of the team doing the preliminary research gave me a lot of confidence. So right there and then, I accepted the challenge.

The old Android search function was just a string-match search. You type in a string of letters, and it finds contacts, text messages, emails and the like that contain a matching string. It was very limited, and could only handle five categories of results. Our intelligent search would give phone users an intelligent, approachable, easy search function that they could access with a single tap. They would not need to open an app. They could just drag down the home page, enter a search query, and get various kinds of results – contacts, messages, news, lifestyle recommendations and more. Then they could get where they wanted to go with just one more tap. There had never been anything like this available from any Android phone maker.

Before we started on the project, no one on the team knew much about desktop search functions. To get the team quickly up to speed, I directed everyone to try out some of the different search functions for themselves. One of the most advanced models out there was the iPhone's Spotlight search function for its iOS system. But we were looking to surpass them with our new intelligent search for Android.

Unfortunately, Apple's iOS is a closed system. No one knows exactly what is going on inside, so there was no way we could build on Apple's search framework. We would have to start from zero.

We sat in the conference room for an entire afternoon, trying things out, making notes and discussing our findings every now and then. This exercise revealed to us a number of problems with existing search functions. For example, existing systems had a narrow search scope and returned few results. They also all took an average of one second to find results, which felt slow and jerky to the user.

Existing engines only offered exact matches, so they couldn't analyse a search into words and then search for those key words. Our analysis showed us where the problems lay, and we determined that our search would be faster, return more results and offer better search functionality.

It used to be that user searches could trawl up a few lonely stars. We wanted our search to serve them constellations on a plate!

The five of us were drawn together from different backgrounds, so I assigned everyone a research goal that matched their skills. I was also very much part of the technical team, researching some of the search basics like search data and consistency of results. Our voyage to the stars was destined to be a bumpy ride, but we were on our way.

Giving everything for an inspired experience

After some discussion, we decided to base our search tool on the built-in search tool in PCs. This choice opened up the next set of options for us, but the PC tool could not simply be copied onto a phone. To make sure that it would work smoothly in the Android environment, it would require a painstaking process of repeated verification and adjustment.

We also spent some time thinking about how our search could return more results than Apple's. First of all, we decided to use Huawei's range of products to our advantage. By introducing results from HUAWEI CLOUD, we were able to increase the variety of our search results. Second, just on the phone itself, Apple's search would only support documents in Apple's own Pages format. We could use the open-source databases Apache Tika and POI to expand our search to common formats like Word, Excel and PowerPoint. This made for a much more useful search process.

We also brought in a tokenizer, which is a tool that breaks up long strings into words for better search results. It took some chopping and updating to make it work in an Android environment.

There were a lot of technical issues to resolve, and we spent nearly a month looking up the technical documentation we needed online, researching the different search algorithms available and matching them to the specific needs of Android. We finally settled on a new search architecture and produced a prototype that would get through minimum viable product (MVP) verification. After a month of working intensively, locked away in the lab, we were now coming up on mid-May, and we had successfully built the new intelligent global search function.

However, just as we were about to present our work, a problem popped up in testing. The search was unable to find content in emails. We spent two days trying to reproduce the same error through stress testing, but couldn't do it. We simply didn't have time in our schedule for this. So to save time, I went through the database operations in the email module myself. In one day, I read close to 20,000 lines of code. By the end of it, I could no longer see straight!

But I finally discovered that under certain circumstances, the email module would bypass the normal database Insert operation. That would result in our search being unable to locate an email even though it had been received. To solve this problem, I had to optimize the email module's parser, and added a process to access its transaction processing. That completely resolved the issue.

The intelligent global search function was added to EMUI 5.0 in early July. It became part of the beta version used for internal testing (open beta testing). But as the beta testing proceeded, our test users began to notice some issues. The search was often slow, and the results were not presented in the most useful order. The system monitors were also showing that the search function was taking up too much memory. It was driving down the performance of the whole phone, and could ultimately lead to a choppy, unresponsive experience for our customers.

Most of the problems could be dealt with quite easily, but tackling the issue of heavy memory use was much harder. We discussed four or five different approaches, such as optimizing or replacing our tokenizer, or delaying indexing, but after trying all of them several times, none of them were getting us the level of performance we needed. I called a meeting with the whole team to discuss the problem, and we came to a consensus: this is something we want to put in the hands of our consumers. There is no room for "good enough." Even if we have to redo everything and start with a whole new architecture, we are going to sort this out, whatever it takes.

In the end, we had to adjust the architecture. We split what was a single application into two separate functions: monitoring and searching. The monitoring function became a lightweight micro service, which was always on but used only a little bit of memory. Its purpose was to monitor data sources for any changes, and make sure the data index was up to date. The search engine itself provided the information, and processed and indexed it. This service would operate only when called, and close when not in use to avoid occupying too much memory for too long.

The two functions were like two people – one stationed on site and one just visiting occasionally to provide support. They worked closely together and it was much more resource-efficient than the original model of having both on site all the time. This solved our beta users' problems.

As a result of our hard work, the intelligent global search function was included in the official release of the Mate 9, one of Huawei's flagship phones. Our search function was able to search through big data ten times more efficiently. It found more than the iOS search could find, both online and within the phone itself, and had an improved tokenizer. It made the Mate 9 a much smarter phone. On 14 November 2016, Huawei Consumer BG CEO Richard Yu officially launched the HUAWEI Mate 9 in Shanghai. When he mentioned the powerful new search function, I cried tears of joy.

I still remember how many hours we spent locked in discussion, selecting components and improving algorithms, just to shave a few dozen milliseconds off the search time, to reduce the memory load by a few megabits, or to return slightly better search results. We solved issue after issue, until finally we were able to give our users the inspired search experience that they deserved. And I now know that it was all worth it.

A young project leader is born

In November 2016, the department head came to talk to me and asked if I would take over as project leader for the contact list team. I had had some experience leading a team in the past, but the contact list team was a big team. Several of the team members had more experience and higher job levels than I did. This team, which produced the phone book or contacts function in our phones, had very high standards for quality. Was I up to the job?

It was a huge challenge, and for a moment I felt daunted. But I remembered what my old professor had said: "Commit to something." He was right. If we don't commit to trying anything, how can we ever really know what is possible and what is not?

In December 2016, I was officially confirmed as the new project leader for the contact list team. We were just starting the new EMUI 8.0 development project. The contacts section is one of the fundamental parts of the operating system, but in previous versions of EMUI, there had been a lot of problems. This meant that we had to keep our people constantly working on maintenance and patches. In addition, the contact list had received quite a few poor ratings in our NPS survey. This told us that a lot of Huawei users were not satisfied with the contact list function, and wanted to see a new function replace it.

The team analysed the problems, and decided that refactoring the architecture was the best approach. However, when resources were first being assigned, the cost–benefit analysis found that refactoring the contact list would generate only marginal returns. Our project was low priority, so we would likely end up being cut from the EMUI 8.0 project. If that happened, R&D would be stuck in a never-ending pattern of patch releases, and phone users would not get the improved experience they deserved.

We were determined not to give up. According to our analysis, the judgements on the value of architectural refactoring were based on some rather woolly estimates. If we wanted to persuade everyone, we would need facts. With this in mind, I sat down with my systems engineers and module design engineers to quantify our refactoring targets. We wanted to put some more detail in the plan, to demonstrate exactly what the value of this refactoring would be, and that the ratio of costs to benefits spoke decisively in favour of doing it. Because our targets were consistent with those of the department head, we got crucial support from him. Thanks to his help, we landed well within the safe zone in the second round of cost–benefit analysis, and were kept on as part of the EMUI 8.0 project.

The refactoring gave us the chance to solve many legacy problems in the old architecture. After the refactoring, the number of trouble tickets fell from 1,207 one year to 307 the next. This was significant in terms of freeing up maintenance engineers. We also created a new selling point, giving our users an exciting new experience through their contact list. The EMUI 8.0 project marked the transformation of the contact list team, and my transformation into a real project leader. The success of the product and the team demonstrated that I was up to the job, and that I could create value in this role.

My three years working here have made me realize that technology will never stop evolving. But our attention to consumer demands must remain as strong as ever. On the road to giving our users an inspired experience, I'm just one little star in the larger galaxy. I may shine weakly, but I'll twinkle as brightly I can. Together, the thousands of young souls like me at Huawei can light the way forward.

A Direct Interaction

By Qiu Xiao

In May, Milan always shimmers with blossoming flowers. There is a canal running through the middle of the city. While travelling down the canal that runs through the middle of the city, you will see numerous Renaissance buildings along both banks. Bars, galleries and antique stores line the waterfront and attract tourists from around the world. In this cultured atmosphere, Huawei was preparing to launch the HUAWEI P8. Everything was ready; we were just waiting for our distinguished guests to arrive.

The weather was fantastic that day, and many Huawei customers and media representatives were due to attend the launch. They were all keen to get their first look at the P8 in Italy. We had arranged some entertainment, a demonstration of the phone and an interactive session. The event drew in crowds from the street, as well as our invited guests.

And me? I was waiting for a girl named Maria, whom I had never met.

Exploring online photography communities

Maria arrived just as dusk was falling. She was a fresh graduate from the Academy of Fine Arts in Naples. Despite her youth, she was the head of the Light Painting Italia association. Why was I waiting for her? Well, it had all started with light painting.

In April 2015, Huawei had just launched its latest flagship phone, the HUAWEI P8. This new phone boasted cameras with disruptive innovations, particularly long-exposure photography and light trails mode. To highlight these features, we arranged an interactive light painting activity at our launch event, so our customers could experience every feature this new phone offered.

The HUAWEI P8 was the first Huawei flagship phone that would be widely available in Italy. Therefore, we planned to open the launch event to the general public. This would be our first time interacting directly with Italian consumers. So what kind of people should we invite? After several rounds of discussion, we decided our main guests should be people who love photography. We started looking for people who matched this description on various social network sites.

We found a Facebook group called Light Painting Italia, which had tens of thousands of members. There were a lot of posts discussing professional photography, particularly light painting. However, most of the active commenters in the group used professional digital SLR cameras. So we wondered if they would even be interested in photos taken using a smartphone camera.

I pretended that I was a photography enthusiast who used a digital SLR camera and joined the group. After a few days of watching the discussions in the group, I learned who the main members were and how they talked to each other. At first, I just started clicking the like button or reposting particularly good photos. Then later, I started posting light paintings taken by one of our P8 ambassadors (a North American photographer). The photos attracted a lot of attention and sparked some long discussions.

We ran a long teaser campaign to build public interest before the launch of the P8 in Italy. During this period, I posted a few more light painting photos in the group, and asked the community to guess what camera was used to take the photos. The images had been captured by professional photographers using the HUAWEI P8, but because of their quality many people thought they had been taken with a professional camera. No one imagined these images could have been taken by a Huawei phone. When the P8 was launched in London, I announced the truth about the photos I had posted, and uploaded a video showing exactly how the photographers had produced these startling images. Everyone in the Light Painting Italia group, which was full of experienced photographers, was shocked that Huawei – then an unknown name – could create such exciting long-exposure images. Some members were even sceptical of the validity of the story, which was understandable.

An incredible response

The HUAWEI P8 would launch in Italy a month later. After months of preparation, I was ready to post an invitation to the launch in the Facebook photography group. I highlighted that we would have interactive light painting at the launch event, which I hoped would attract the attention of these light painting fans. However, the response was quite underwhelming, and most of comments I received were noncommittal. The group's members were scattered all over Italy, and they did not seem to believe the event was exciting enough to warrant taking the long journey to Milan.

I wondered if this was because Huawei was not a big enough brand, we weren't perceived to be high quality or simply because the group members disliked phone cameras. Whatever the reason, the group's reaction was mild at best, and made me feel frustrated.

But a few days later, a woman named Maria responded to my post, bringing it back to the front page of the group. She commented, "I am going to be visiting Milan, and I would like to go to the P8 launch event. Do I need to bring anything?" I was elated when I saw this response, and immediately contacted her and provided her with the programme and every detail of the event.

On the evening of the launch event, I met Maria and showed her the HUAWEI P8 in great detail. I invited her to our interactive zone, and took a photo of her in light trails mode using the P8. The light painting looked perfect against a deep blue sky. When she saw how I had painted angel wings on her in light, she thought it looked fantastic. As the event came to an end, she said she was very grateful that I had invited her along. However, when I asked her whether she was interested in buying a P8, she just smiled and said nothing.

Two months later, Maria posted a picture of her brand-new HUAWEI P8, fresh out of its box, on a social network site. She wrote, "A generous invitation deserves a sincere response." Ever since, Maria has been a firm fan of the HUAWEI P series. She often posts light painting photos that she has taken with her P8.

The launch of the P8 was a milestone for Huawei, and did a lot to help familiarize Italian customers with our brand and products; 2015 saw a significant increase in Huawei's share in the smartphone market. Huawei became one of the top three smartphone brands in Italy, and has grown rapidly since then.

Ambassador for Huawei's Talent Programme

In 2016, Huawei launched the P9, which featured the Leica dual-lens camera. Great products will always find their own market, and the P9 was no exception, quickly gaining a large fan base in Italy. Maria had already been delighted with the amazing camera on the P8, so how could she ignore the new Leica dual-lens camera?

Sure enough, she soon purchased the HUAWEI P9 Plus. The Leica dual-lens camera didn't disappoint her. She posted a number of beautiful light painting photos in the Facebook group. Following encouragement from Maria, some other group members also started trying Huawei smartphones.

As the head of the Light Painting Italia, Maria sometimes organized photography get-togethers. When she saw the excellent results achieved using a Huawei camera for light painting, she organized several light painting events specifically focused on the use of Huawei phones.

Many of the group members who did light painting were accustomed to using digital SLR cameras, and they were still unsure about using a smartphone for light painting. However, Maria's posts gave them the chance to learn about Huawei phones. Gradually, they came to realize how good Huawei's long-exposure mode was, and more group members were slowly converted into loyal Huawei users. Maria became more than just another Huawei customer, and she was almost like a member of the team. We were becoming firm friends, despite only knowing each other for one year.

In 2017, the HUAWEI P10 and Mate 10 were the year's most popular new phones. The Huawei name was everywhere – on the TV and radio programmes, in the news, top magazines and tech interviews.

Launch of the HUAWEI Mate 10 Pro, displayed on Europe's largest outdoor screen – Milan, Italy

In 2017, the HUAWEI P10 and Mate 10 were the year's most popular new phones. The Huawei name was everywhere – on the TV and radio programmes, in the news, top magazines and tech interviews

When the HUAWEI P10 was launched, we also initiated a Talent Programme in Italy. This programme was based on the idea that every person with talent and vision deserves a chance to take on new challenges and realize their dreams. The programme was aligned with one of Huawei's slogans: Make It Possible. During the programme, Huawei consumers showed off their talents and stories by uploading videos, pictures and other forms of media. We then prepared to select five talent ambassadors from the entries, and each of these ambassadors would be given a HUAWEI P10 Plus as a prize. The programme gave us a lot more exposure in Italy, and as soon as it began, we received a flood of entries from talented individuals, including artists, musicians, dancers and athletes.

It was a lovely surprise to find our old friend Maria taking part in the talent programme as well. We decided to feature her light painting photographs on the front pages of our social network sites several times. As a result, she became one of our five talent ambassadors. Now she was truly a part of the Huawei family.

My last meeting with Maria was in early March 2018. She happened to be in Milan and I invited her to visit our first flagship experience store in Europe. The experience store combined Chinese technology with an Italian sense of style, creating a harmonious, environmentally friendly and high-tech experience. Maria was very complimentary about it!

I suggested that we pose for a photo together in the store, so a group of us stood holding the invitation letter to the P8 launch and a promotional picture of the P20. We had now known each other for three years since the launch of the HUAWEI P8 in 2015. Maria had witnessed the evolution of Huawei phones and how they had improved, and was now a loyal user. And each generation of Huawei phones had lived up to her expectations thanks to their innovative features. The phones often inspired her photographic creativity.

A light painting photo taken by Maria for Valentine's Day
using the HUAWEI P10 Plus

"You are virtually a brand ambassador," I said, as Maria was about to leave.

"Thank you for the invitation back in 2015," she replied. "I had never heard of Huawei, but you introduced the brand to me and gave me the opportunity to learn about it. I bought the P8 out of curiosity, but I bought the P9 and the P10 because of the brand and Huawei's high quality."

Huawei's Italian team has been working on building the Huawei brand for years. We are reaching out to more consumers, helping them understand, recognize and trust Huawei, and bringing them better products, sales experiences and post-sales experiences. Like Maria, most people only have to try Huawei once before becoming lifelong fans.

Maria at Huawei's first flagship experience shop in Europe

By 2017, Huawei was one of the 100 best-known consumer brands in Italy, and the only Chinese brand to make it into this list. Now, Huawei is a major brand in Italy, and is well known and well liked across the country. As our market share has continued to increase, Huawei has become one of Italy's best-loved high-end phone brands.

The Dumbest Bird in the Flock Takes Flight

By Zhao Ming

Undoing one more button

Dusseldorf is always cold in the spring, and early spring of 2015 was no exception. I had just finished a 10 km run, and when I took out my phone to check my email, one subject line jumped out at me: "Ken Hu wants to see you urgently. Please call back ASAP." I didn't know it at the time, but this email would move me onto a whole new path. My future, and the future of the Honor brand, were about to become a lot more unpredictable.

It was during one of Ken Hu's terms as rotating CEO. When I got through to him on the phone, Ken Hu wasted no time: "The board has decided to make you the CEO of Honor." He also joked that the board had had some doubts about the appointment, and that Mr Ren had even asked, "Isn't Zhao Ming a bit too strait-laced?" But Ken Hu had put in a word for me: "He's the man for the job."

When Ken told me this, my reaction was somewhat mixed. For me, this job would clearly be a major challenge. In the back of my mind, I was wondering why they had chosen me. This was a job in which the only acceptable result was success. Did I have the ability to pull it off? Could I make a difference to Honor? I was feeling hesitant, and asked Ken if I could have a moment to think about it. An hour later, I called him back with my answer.

"Good," he replied. "Remember, this is a public position, so be prepared."

That evening, the press release and open letter were prepared, and the next day the company formally announced my new position to the world. That same day, I had a long video conference with the Honor team to talk about the business. I still had some loose ends to tie up in my old job, so I was unable to return to China immediately. For the first two weeks, I met with my new team through video calls only. I thought we would have a quiet transition period, but as it turned out, just two weeks later I would be put to the test at the Mobile World Congress (MWC) in Barcelona.

At MWC, we were launching the Honor X2 and the Honor router, as scheduled. The day before the event, I rushed from Germany over to Spain so that I could be at the launch. When I arrived, Richard Yu, the CEO of Huawei's Consumer BG, suddenly said to me, "Ming, you're the CEO of Honor now. I think you should do the product launch tomorrow." I was astonished, but I also didn't have any way to back out of it. This was my responsibility now.

I was tense, not because I didn't know the products, but because I had never spoken to the mass media before. I had never launched a product. At that moment, it hit me like a tidal wave: helming Honor would be very different from anything I had ever done before.

The next day, just before I went on stage, I took off my jacket, unknotted my tie and stepped out in shirtsleeves. I even undid another button on my shirt. They say that this represents the openness and freedom of the internet industry, but I was the butt of my colleagues' jokes for months because of those open buttons.

Team stability is vital for victory

Five days after the MWC product launch, I finally returned to China, and was able to fully dedicate my time to Honor.

There had been a lot of changes at Honor as 2015 was a year of shake-ups. The first thing I had to do was to stop the constant change and settle my team. What's the best way to do that? Make it a winning team. It was then the end of March, and a lot of our competitors were cutting their prices and launching big sales. What could we do to steal momentum from our rivals?

We spent three days and nights locked in discussion over this question. The consensus was that we shouldn't do what everyone else was doing. We needed to forge our own path. My years of experience in overseas markets told me that Honor's key strength is the global reach our parent company gives us. We could use our global markets to outperform our competitors. At that point Honor phones were already available in more than 70 different countries. If we could find a way to combine the strengths of these different markets, we would be a force to be reckoned with. That turned into the idea for the Global Sales Festival on 8 April.

Come 8 April, we launched a sale in all of our global markets simultaneously. It showed our Chinese customers that the Honor brand had real global strength. This was a Chinese brand that was very different from any other online phone vendor. The 8 April sale got us off to a good start. We got reports of strong sales from all around the world. But it was not enough to raise the morale of the Honor team. The next big challenge was going to be the 18 June sale. For Chinese online phone brands, 18 June was one of the two big sales pushes every year. We would need to deliver good enough results to settle the Honor team.

To be honest, if Honor tried to compete on price alone, we would have a difficult time. Huawei invests a lot in R&D, and we can't pay that kind of investment back with losses. We thought about compromising on profit: we could accept a few short-term losses in exchange for some good figures. We weren't after the sales themselves; we just needed to generate some headlines. Many of my colleagues were keen on this idea. But what next? Once the losses gouged a big hole in our balance sheet, how would we fill it? Everyone knows that we can't sell at low prices forever. So why not choose a better path from the start? Huawei's advantage is that we are able to offer quality built on our 30 years of experience. So, we worked out a way to turn that quality into value. On 18 June, when everyone else was slashing prices, Huawei made an offer to consumers: we'll give you a year-long warranty for just one yuan.

Back then, the markets still viewed online-only phone brands with a great deal of scepticism, so this offer of a warranty was a shocking move.

We were ready to move a serious number of phones on 18 June 2015.

But there were more unpredictable challenges in store for us. In the run up to 18 June, there was a freak accident with one of the trucks delivering a container full of Honor phones. One of the tyres overheated and caught fire. Fortunately, the flames never got to any of the phones inside. A few got overheated because of the fire, but most were completely unaffected, without so much as a smudge on their packaging, and the phones proved to be completely functional on testing. Our quality department told us that most of these phones would be fine for a minimum of two years. But they couldn't give us a 100% guarantee that the phones had no quality issues. So, what could we do with these phones? We were talking about a shipment of more than 17,000 phones, with a total value of about ¥20 million. These were some of our most popular models, and were very much needed to stop our warehouses from running out of stock. Could we sell them at a reduced price, with an explanation to the customers, to mitigate our losses? The Honor management team decided that as a growing brand, we had to put quality first. The only way we could make good on our responsibility to our customers was to insist on the very highest standards of quality.

Public destruction of ¥20 million of Honor phones, 2015

Quality is a matter of self-respect for Honor, and we had to make sure that our products' quality continued to be our most unimpeachable spokesperson. Honor was determined to provide products of a quality equal to or better than Japanese and German brands. This was a necessity for us, and that's why we realized we had to work harder than everyone else. In this case, what that meant was that we decided to destroy the entire shipment of phones.

The news that Honor was destroying 20 million yuan worth of phones quickly spread through the industry and out into the public consciousness. Suddenly, the lengths to which Honor was prepared to go to in the pursuit of quality became a powerful piece of publicity that would drive sales for us during the annual 18 June shopping festival rush. Our one-yuan warranty was another clear demonstration of our belief in the quality of our phones. And the result was that, in 2015, Honor became the best-selling online-only phone in the 18 June sales.

Our success in the 18 June sale galvanized the Honor brand. From that point on, our momentum seemed unstoppable. In October, we hit our 2015 sales target of US$5 billion. That meant we had fully met our key performance indicator (KPI) goal with a cool two months to spare. It was a moment of exhilaration, but we were also thinking about how to ensure big numbers in the 11 November shopping festival sale. My team had a suggestion: give something back to our customers. What could we give them? That was easy – money!

Honor decided that our customers should receive an annual bonus. If our sales revenue hit our annual target, we would give our customers ¥100 million back. Based on our sales projections, that meant hundreds of millions of yuan would be going back to our users. This giveback would happen between November 2015 and February 2016, so it would include all sales made in the big 11 November sale, as well as in the 12 December, Christmas, New Year and Chinese New Year sales. It meant that the more we sold, the more we would give away. This strategy captured the imaginations of our target market.

As a result, the 11 November sales were pretty much a foregone conclusion. Honor easily took the crown as the biggest online seller. What we didn't yet know was that this giveaway would help us win the loyalty of our customers in the following sixth months when we faced greater difficulties.

Rebuilding after a rocky start

Honor brought 2015 to a close in a storm of positive reviews. We had had an incredible year, and were clearly the big story of 2015 among online phone brands. In my annual appraisal, I got the A grade that everyone at Huawei always wants so badly. But my team and I knew that under this lovely exterior, Honor had problems to be solved. If we took our eye off the ball for a minute, everything we'd achieved could all come crashing down around us.

At the end of 2015, as an extension of its dual brand strategy, the Consumer BG announced that Honor would be managed completely independently from then on. Honor's retail and routes to market would be separated from those of our powerful patron. We would have to start our own offline retail sales from nothing. Our online store on Tmall (one of China's biggest online marketplaces) would be split from Huawei's. When this happened, we experienced an instant 40% drop in sales. Our retail channels were hit hard as well. The birth of our retail strategy was accompanied by all the usual rethinks and birth pains. It was like being a start-up all over again.

But there was nothing to say about that: Honor was to be independent. This was a necessary step, decided at the company's highest level. So, we were on our own. We couldn't rely on the Huawei brand anymore; and we didn't have to play second fiddle to Huawei anymore. We were choosing our own path now.

The young Honor team was champing at the bit. If we weren't to get a ready-made route to the retail market, then they were raring to go out and build our own. If we no longer had our own sales channel team, well then everyone would get out there and do the sales themselves. The way we said it internally was: when the revolution comes, even a cook puts himself on the front line. Why not us? We could do everything from fan clubs and go-to-market to marketing on the ground, getting our new team up and running.

One day I was visiting the city of Zhengzhou to check out their market situation. "You don't have an office here," I remarked to the local sales guy. "Where do you work?"

He was very relaxed about it. He gave a belly laugh and said, "It's only me here! Who needs a one-man office?"

"What if you have to meet a customer?"

"We go and sit in a McDonald's. It's clean, and they have good air conditioning in the summer." Then he thought for a moment, and said, "There is one bad thing: the staff keep moving us around."

The Honor sales channels were built up from every possible location

Honor is forever young, forever passionate and forever committed to surpassing ourselves.

That was the situation as we were developing our brick-and-mortar retail strategy. Today, we sell as many phones through retail stores as we do online. This has given us an excellent basis for fast, ongoing sales growth, and it was all down to the determination of our first group of sales people, who didn't hesitate even when they had only a McDonald's to do business in.

In 2016, the new separate status of Honor meant that staff turnover started to rise once again. Key people like the sales and services director and product general manager had to be replaced, and all the changes hindered our ability to build relationships with our partners. In one case, a customer had agreed to take 500,000 phones, but by the time we had got the stock ready, they had changed their minds and refused to collect it. All of the changes were wearing us down and leaving us unable to get it together. That year everyone was constantly asking, "How can we stop this?"

It was hard restarting our business. In 2016, every potential problem that could have occurred did occur. But I had foreseen this possibility well in advance. At the end of 2015, whenever anyone congratulated me for a successful year, I would always say, "If there's anyone willing to take my job, I'll give it to them straightaway. This is not an easy job."

The bigger problem that we ran into in 2016 was a lack of products. We were in the world of online phone sales, but we had to sell a single model for 20 months straight. Between 28 October 2015 and 28 April 2016, we had a six-month period without any new product releases.

Originally, we had planned to launch the Honor 7 Plus in December 2015. It was to have the dual-camera system, but the new dual-camera design wasn't ready in time. If we went ahead with the launch on the planned date, there was no way we could put dual cameras on the phone. That left us with effectively no choice at all. Everyone agreed that we wanted to give our customers the best technologies and products available, and that meant dual cameras. Unfortunately, that turned out to mean waiting for a full six months.

And when the time came, half a year later, we were in an even more embarrassing position. Come May, we would be launching the new model – the Honor 8. If the 7 Plus and the 8 were launched that close together, it would only confuse our customers.

But, sometimes, the toughest situations breed the brightest ideas. We simply changed the name of the 7 Plus to the V8, and it became one of our biggest successes! It also became the first in a whole new product line: the Honor V series.

In 2016, there was a lot of argument within the company about the future of Honor. But in the second half of the year, Honor put itself firmly back in the spotlight. The Honor 8 was one of the superstar phones of the year, and the Honor 6X was a top seller in the 11 November sale. On that day alone, we sold hundreds of thousands of units. Tmall described the 6X as another "super cool" product from Honor.

Honor had a heavy burden to carry, but we were committed. At our end-of-year review meeting, we had not hit our fast growth target. I received a B as my personal performance grade that year. But at the end of the year, I had more confidence than I had ever felt since taking over the job. Honor had built its own retail sales network. We had our own superstar products. We had our own personality as a brand. In the past, our skills had always been put at the service of other people. Now we held our fate in our own hands.

At the end of 2016, I pleaded with the company leadership: give me a C if you want, just don't move me out of Honor now. I was determined to stay on at Honor, because I was confident that 2017 would be the year Honor would really take off.

Top online phone brand

In 2017, our year started in the second month of the Chinese calendar, and it was an excellent start. Our sales were stunning. The Honor 6X displayed its strength once again, and flew off the shelves, leaving domestic e-commerce companies astonished. On 21 February, another blockbuster appeared – the Honor V9 – and that boosted our sales up to another level once again. The V9 became our leader. Our customers, looking at its powerful specifications, called the V9 a "beast."

This was Honor's real lift off. In 2017, we were secure atop the leaderboard for online phone brands, and the brand had great momentum within the Chinese market.

This was our moment to make a decisive play for market share in the global market.

In June 2017, we announced our plan to double our sales by growing our overseas base. It was an inspiring vision, but making it happen was not so simple. How could we build up our own sales channels overseas? How could we set our own rules of the game? This was the big challenge for Honor.

Openness, collaboration, learning and progression
– these are the base pairs of Honor's DNA

Honor was, for many years, dependent on Huawei and its overseas sales network, and our imaginations had become rather constrained. Faced with making choices for ourselves, we got off to a difficult start. One of our sales managers in Country Y said to me: "In this country we just have to keep following Huawei's strategy. If we keep going, we will succeed." But we thought that if Honor just copied the Huawei model, we'd never carve out our own place. However, we couldn't persuade the sales manager and, in the end, we decided to let the man on the ground lead the fight. Much as we predicted, the outcome was mediocre sales.

Building a sales network from scratch, and disagreements over strategy – the situation was very similar to the early beginnings of Honor in China in previous years. But everyone was excited that, this year, we were setting the rules and shaping the markets.

After we adjusted our strategy in Country Y and returned to Honor's own asset-light, online strategy, 2018 got off to a roaring start. In the very first quarter of the year, we recorded a 300% increase in sales. Honor sales outside China doubled.

Now Honor was firmly on the right road, both inside China and globally. With its great products and high sales figures, Honor had proven itself to be indomitable.

Pioneering, experimenting and trailblazing

Since 2015, Honor has been experimenting and blazing a new trail for Huawei. Honor was the first to put dual cameras on a phone. We were the first to power a phone with a Kirin chip. With the Honor Magic, we were the first to launch an AI phone. And we were the first to operate under a dual model with both online and offline sales. At the end of 2017, Mr Ren personally signed off on a new bonus policy. Once again, Honor was to be the pioneer, this time in our Human Resources and organizational operations. And 2018 was the breakout year for AI. It seems hard to imagine that in 2015, when we were launching the Magic and the V10 – two AI smartphones – other phone makers in China were having concerns about the use of AI. So far as we can tell, we were one of the earliest adopters of AI phones in the market.

When I had just arrived at Honor, the team and I sat and considered a new question: what is Honor's unique strength? We didn't have the marketing skills that some companies have. We weren't skilled in telling our story. So, our unique skill was not marketing.

Finally, we decided that our three strategic capabilities were quality, innovation and service. Later that year, at the Global Mobile Internet Conference (GMIC) 2015, we heard the story of the dumbest bird in the flock. They say that when the wind gets strong enough, even pigs start flying. But Huawei was not a pig, dependent on the strong winds. We were an early bird – in fact, the dumbest bird in the flock. When the winds die down, the pig falls out the sky. But a bird can fly on the power of its own wings, and even the dumbest bird keeps flapping its wings, no matter what. With our three core strengths, we could base our future strategy on our quality, service and innovation, and just keep flapping our wings!

At the end of December 2017, Honor held its annual meeting somewhat early. The slogan of that meeting expressed nicely what we intended to do: "A new start for Honor: aiming for the global market while defending our position in the low-end market." After the toasts, when the dinner was supposed to be drawing to an end, people somehow weren't leaving the restaurant. Colleagues who would be setting off for new countries hugged and wished each other luck. There was not a dry eye in the house, but I knew that every one of them was determined to succeed on their new battle-fields. Because being young means being full of energy.

Honor is forever young, forever passionate and forever committed to surpassing ourselves.

The
Indomitable
Team

By Wang Yanmin

When I was clearing out the files on my computer the other day, I found a plan that I made back in 2014 when I was new to the regional office in Northern, Central and Eastern Europe (NCEE). In the plan, we aimed to double our smartphone sales in five years. At that time, many thought our targets were impossible. No one could have imagined that it would only take us three years to hit the five-year target, as our market share exploded. I often ask myself, how did we pull it off? After going over the whole process in my mind again, I've realized that there is only one answer: it was our people who made it possible. They were a wonderful group of people – some fiery, some more reserved, all unique – and they dedicated the best years of their lives to achieving this remarkable success.

Kevin Li: the man who threatened to jump into the Danube

Austria used to be one of Huawei's best markets. In 2008, cellular dongles alone were generating very good revenue for us in Austria. But, somehow, smartphone sales had been sluggish. Kevin Li was appointed the Austria General Manager for the Consumer BG in 2014. This was a promotion from his old position of sales manager – but not much of a promotion. There was actually only one other person on his team, who was in charge of testing and certification. Kevin had no people, no money and no resources, so he ended up with no revenue or profit, and nothing to invest in marketing.

One day in 2015, I was shocked to learn from a co-worker that Kevin was going to jump into a river. I rushed to call Kevin, only to hear him laugh at the other end of the line. "I didn't mean that literally!" he explained. "I just meant I'm diving into a challenge."

Austria is a mature market. Consumers there are very selective about foreign brands. Kevin was fighting to find a way in, but potential customers kept telling him that working with a new brand was too much of a risk for them. There was too much uncertainty about the market demand for Huawei, which was not well known at that time, and was not investing much in branding. In fact, our regional office in NCEE was no more optimistic than the customers. They had never seen big phone sales in Austria, so they thought that investing in branding there would just be a waste of money. They weren't willing to take the chance, so our branding spending had been low for years.

Kevin was not discouraged. He spent a lot of time doing market surveys and visiting customers. He predicted that branding investment in Austria would pay off handsomely. After careful deliberation, he invited colleagues from the regional office in NCEE to visit Austria, see the sales outlets and market, and survey the major billboard campaigns being run by our competitors. They talked late into the night, and when they were finally heading back to the hotel, they walked by the River Danube. The winters in Europe are long, and though it was already April, the air was still chilly along the river. It didn't feel like spring at all yet. Kevin said, "Please approve my budget, and let me build our brand. If we don't hit our sales targets next year, I will jump into the Danube in front of you." Kevin's face showed that he was dead serious.

Kevin later told me on the phone, "Customers are ready to work with Huawei. They are optimistic about our P8. Shouldn't we be more optimistic? If we invest enough, I don't think I will need to jump into the river – our customers will deliver the results." Kevin's passion and sense of mission were contagious. His business case was strong and convincing. So I approved his application for a bigger budget in Austria.

Kevin soon launched an ad campaign across many of Austria's major landmarks, including ads in the Vienna International Airport and opposite the Musikverein, Vienna's most famous concert hall. He also ran several weeks of commercials on major TV networks with a limited budget. Customers later told him that they were impressed by Huawei's strong brand marketing and the swift rollout of the campaign.

Their efforts paid off. Huawei finally cracked open the market and gained a significant market share. The banks of the Danube began glowing with Huawei red!

Their efforts paid off.
Huawei finally cracked
open the market and
gained a significant
market share. The banks
of the Danube began
glowing with Huawei red!

Little Prince Yan: collision with an elk

With a population of more than eight million, Austria is unusual for NCEE. More common here are smaller countries, with a population of one or two million, like Lithuania, Latvia and Estonia.

Yan, who for some reason was always known as the Little Prince, was in charge of the Baltics. In 2015, when I moved him there from Bulgaria, the Baltic team had only six members, and the Little Prince was the only one from China.

One day in 2016, the Little Prince had just left from a meeting with a customer in the evening, when he received a phone call from an executive of a telecom operator in Lithuania, inviting him to talk about a potential deal at 9 a.m. the next day.

This was the largest telecom operator in Lithuania, and it had never sold Huawei phones before. Our people had visited them a few times, but had only been able to secure meetings with procurement managers – never with the CEO. So Yan was excited about the chance to sit down with their CEO. It was already evening, but he jumped in his car and headed straight to Vilnius, Lithuania, over 300 km away. He didn't even stop to eat; he just set off along the deserted roads through the forest in the darkness of the night.

As he drove along the bumpy road, he suddenly heard a bang. Startled, he stepped on the brake and realized that his car had hit an elk crossing the road. He got out of the car and found that the front fog lamp was smashed, the front bumper was broken, and the splash shield under the engine was about to fall off. Yan was too shocked to worry about his condition or his car; he was more worried about the elk. If the elk did not survive the crash, there could be legal consequences in the Baltics. Yan prayed that the elk would be all right. He examined the animal closely, but it did not seem to be injured – just knocked out by the impact. Yan sat in the car for a while. Then the elk slowly stood up and then ran off. "Thank God!" Yan breathed a sigh of relief, and continued driving his damaged car until he made it to Vilnius at midnight.

The next day Yan put on his suit and tie, and drove his broken car to the customer's office. He told the CEO his elk story. The CEO laughed out loud, and before long, he had signed his company's first contract with Huawei. Just before Christmas,

Huawei's P series smartphones were stocked in all the operator's outlets, and sales soared.

Yan's car racked up over 170,000 km in the Baltic States in just a few years. He joked that his car was his mobile office. In the next two years, the P series posted strong sales in the Baltics, even though the three countries combined have fewer than six million people.

Language savant Seth Wang: learning Turkish in five months

Seth was transferred to Huawei's regional office in NCEE from Brazil in 2015. In 2017, he was appointed director of Turkey Device Business Department. The management was hoping that he could make a breakthrough in this difficult market.

Before he assumed his new post, I asked him what his plan was.

"As a new player in the market, we should talk to the customers in a way they understand," he said. "We have to adapt to our market."

I did not know at the time that by "adapting" he meant learning Turkish so that he could talk to the customers. Then he actually did it.

Seth started to spend time learning Turkish every day on top of his busy job. He found a local tutor to help him correct his mistakes in grammar, vocabulary, pronunciation and intonation. He would practise over and over, late into the night. Five months later, it was time to put his Turkish to the test.

Huawei invited its Turkish distributors to a conference. Seth was going to give a speech in Turkish in front of more than 3,000 people. Many of the team members were worried about what might happen, but Seth remained confident. At the conference, he gave a fluent speech, interrupted by applause seven times. Our customers were very impressed that a Chinese vendor with no Turkish background managed to give a talk in fluent Turkish in a mere five months. They recognized his commitment and sincerity, and saw it as a reflection of Huawei's commitment to the country. That opened the door to the Turkish market for Huawei.

After his speech, Seth became a mini-celebrity in the Turkey office. But that was not the first time he had learned a new language.

During his time in Brazil, he had also taught himself fluent Portuguese. I asked why he always learned the local language, and he told me that he just had to. He thought it was easier to build trust with customers when you speak their language. It enables you to discuss with them in more depth, he said. Be it in Brazil or Turkey, he used the local language whenever he could, whether it was going to the supermarket to buy nappies (diapers) for his baby, or talking to local consumers to get feedback on Huawei phones. He practised the language while getting the job done. He was so good at learning new languages that I thought he must be a linguist by training, but later I learned that he had studied sciences at university. His ability to learn new languages rapidly earned him the nickname of "language savant," and played a decisive role in his success in Turkey.

At the year-end banquet in 2018, Seth had a fair amount to drink. In the car on the way home, he suddenly burst into tears. I asked why he was crying when we were doing such great business in Turkey. He told me that he was crying tears of joy – the success had been hard won. Indeed, without his hard work and perseverance, it would not have been possible.

Thor Gotz: the thunder god in Denmark

In 2016, Richard Yu, CEO of the Consumer BG, left me a voice message, asking, "Where did you get the money to pay for the advertisement in Nyhavn?" I was getting rather worried, wondering what the problem was, when I received a follow-up message: "The Huawei logo looks great over the landmark! An old school friend of mine saw the Huawei logo at this tourist spot and took a photo to send to me. He was excited to see a familiar brand there and felt very proud."

Nyhavn [New Harbour] is the longest promenade in Europe. It's very near to Copenhagen's Kongens Nytorv [King's New Square]. There are many brightly coloured houses, bars, canteens and coffee shops dating back to the 17th century. Now, the Huawei logo can be seen in the most prominent position, right between the Kongens Nytorv and Nyhavn. An advertisement in this location reaches more than just Danish audiences: every year, around

50 million foreign tourists visit Denmark, including 300,000 from China. This precious advertising space was secured by Thor Gotz, our resident thunder god in the land of Hans Christian Andersen.

Thor was previously a salesman working for one of our customers. He joined Huawei as a junior sales manager and, step by step, he advanced up the ranks to become Huawei's Device Sales Director for Denmark. When I went on a business trip to Denmark in 2015, Thor told me, "Over 50% of the people in Denmark use iPhones, and most of the rest use Samsung phones. Success will not come easy for a new entrant like Huawei. To deliver extraordinary results, we will have to put in extraordinary efforts."

"What extraordinary efforts are you talking about?" I asked.

"Like installing our logo in the highest-traffic areas to promote our brand," replied Thor.

This was a bold idea. For starters, it was difficult to install anything on landmark buildings because they were heavily regulated. But a few months later, I received a call from Thor: "Mr Wang, we secured advertising space on a landmark building in Nyhavn! We made it!" He was as excited as a kid.

We had luck on our side. Government approval was required in order to install a logo on a building in this area. We secured government approval to put the Huawei logo on the Copenhagen Amber Museum, but at the time the advertising space was already occupied by another brand. Our people from the Denmark office paid a visit to the manager of the Copenhagen Amber Museum to ask if we could buy out the contract. We told him we were willing to pay more. But the manager declined our offer, saying that it was not about money. This prominent location, he said, was reserved for major international brands, and Huawei was not one of them (at least not according to the average person in Denmark). Besides, he had already signed a long-term contract with the existing brand.

But we did not lose hope. We waited for an opportunity and, in October 2015, an opportunity came when we learned that the contract with the existing brand was expiring. We immediately went to the owner of the property. The 80-year-old was hesitant because he still thought that Huawei did not seem like a big brand.

We told him, "There are already many people in Denmark using Huawei's products and services. Huawei has been supplying telecom operators in Denmark with telecommunication gear and consumer devices for years. The 4G cellular towers that enable mobile communication, for example, come from Huawei. We have kept a low profile, but we are a major brand. Our products and services are now woven into the fabric of daily life here. It would be quite something if you could allow a low-key brand like us to present ourselves to the general public."

The owner laughed and agreed to our proposal.

The logo in Nyhavn was only the beginning of our branding campaign in Denmark. As we continued to communicate our brand, awareness of Huawei smartphones reached an all-time high. In 2017, Huawei was recognized as the fastest-growing brand in Denmark by YouGov, a leading market research firm.

This strong performance would not have been possible without the hard work of many local employees like Thor. Living 100 km away from the office, Thor spent four hours every day commuting, but that did not stop him from working late into the night with the rest of the team. Thor did not even allow holidays to interrupt his work – he would reply to emails immediately, whatever the time was, wherever he was.

The Huawei logo on top of a landmark in Denmark

Thor (right) and Richard Yu

Conclusion

We have a diverse team in NCEE, and I often feel inspired by them. They hail from the coast of the Baltic Sea to the Aegean Sea, from the Black Sea to Austria, Hungary, Turkey and Finland. They speak different languages, but all share the same determination and resilience, moving forward one step at a time in spite of any difficulties. Together, they helped forged Huawei's enormous success across Northern Europe.

Invisible Security for Your Money

By Gao Jujia and Chang Xinmiao

It is commonplace today to make payments and transfer money online. Many of us are familiar with inserting a USB dongle into the computer to make large payments and transfers. Now, phones are starting to displace computers as our device of choice for online banking services, and mobile finance is a fast-growing sector. But security remains a key worry. Regulators, banks, third-party service providers, phone manufacturers, solutions providers … A whole constellation of industries is busy thinking about how to guarantee that consumers can access financial services on their mobile devices easily and securely.

In October 2017, Huawei launched the Mate 10, the first phone with a built-in security key. This was a vital step in solving these security issues: a phone with a built-in security key is as good as putting a padlock on your mobile payments.

The first security key

In the last few years, there have been many security incidents around mobile payments. The People's Bank of China (PBoC), China's highest-level financial regulator, has driven the widespread adoption of hardware security technologies like Trusted Execution Environment (TEE) and Security Element (SE) to protect mobile financial services. The China Financial Certification Authority (CFCA) is the most authoritative provider of electronic certification for the financial sector, and is one of the pioneers for mobile financial security. We spoke many times with the CFCA, and realized that hardware security for mobile payments must be based ultimately on the underlying security capabilities and technologies that phones already have. Huawei has a very good understanding of these technologies, and was well positioned to develop technologies that supported the secure environment required by the PBoC, and could be certified by the CFCA. This meant that the security key function could be built directly into our phones, delivering exactly the same standard of security as the USB dongles that you plug into a computer.

For Huawei, the security key was a step into uncharted territory. Back then, the dongle system was dominated by giant chip makers and SIM card makers, from the domestic to the international markets.

So, developing an internal security key was always going to be a challenge for the Huawei R&D engineers.

In March 2016, we established a project team for the phone security key. Looking back on the old days of the R&D project, Xu, a colleague from the Software Security Engineering Department, said that we were flying blind, working everything out as we went along. The security key was an entirely new product, and we only had the first glimmerings of an idea. No one knew what problems we would encounter during development.

We progressed step by step, and the development phase actually went fairly smoothly. But at this point we encountered a problem: the security key was not a single product. It had to interface with three separate operating systems – the phone's Android system, the TEE and the card operating system (COS). When we called the security key function, the Android system would receive the command, which it would pass on to the TEE. Once the TEE had finished its processing, it would pass on the result to the COS, and the sequence would come to an end there. However, the TEE could only execute processes in a single thread. The algorithms involved were sometimes quite time-consuming, and while the phone would be preoccupied with processing them, it couldn't do anything else but wait for the TEE to finish. To put it in simple terms, when you were using the security key, the screen would suddenly black out. You would have to unlock the phone again with your fingerprint, but while the security key was still finishing its process, the fingerprint scanner would be unable to work, so there would be no way to wake the phone up at all.

The discovery of this problem killed our elation at having completed the early-phase development so quickly. We scrambled to get in touch with our colleagues at HiSilicon, Huawei's chip arm, so that we could think about how to handle the issue together. It took two full days of intense discussion. The whiteboard in the conference room was filled up and erased, then filled up and erased again. It felt like a thousand times. Finally, we worked out a solution with the minimum level of risk: we would optimize the TEE, so that it was able to handle multiple commands simultaneously. This sounds simple enough when you say it, but it required a massive push by every member of the project team. We came to a very clear understanding of that old bit of wisdom: greatness comes from hard work.

But we did manage to solve the technical issues one by one, until our new TEE was ready to pass its stress tests. Now our security key was finally ready.

Hammering out a new standard

Phone security is a very new area, but it is crucial for maintaining the security of our customers' financial transactions, so the whole industry is watching eagerly for new developments. Both regulators and industry players thought that we needed to develop standards to put the industry on a more consistent and healthier development path. We also thought that standards would reassure our customers: if Huawei's security key was compliant with the industry standard, and had certification from the financial regulators, customers could use it with more confidence.

In early 2016, the PBoC assembled an inter-agency working group to develop a standard for trusted payment environments via mobile devices. Industry representatives included Huawei, CFCA, China Financial Authentication, Alibaba, Tencent, Beanpod Technology and several banks. Our discussions focused on how to integrate the TEE and SE technologies into a phone to create a trusted environment for payments, and how to describe that in a standard. The standard would become *Mobile Device Payment Trusted Environment Specification*.

We started with nothing but a blank sheet of paper. Where should we start in developing an architecture for this standard? For a while, everyone was stuck. The problem was that the security key would need to involve everyone: phone makers, digital certification bodies, banks and so on. We were one of the lead drafters, so Huawei made one of the first proposals: the standard should be divided into two parts. The first would be the steps involved in the implementation of the security key; the second would be the security requirements for the systems within which the security key is embedded. Splitting the standard like this would be very useful in terms of setting clear roles for banks, phone makers and other participants. We would be able to clearly distinguish the different standards that each participant would need to apply and comply with.

The working group included all of the key players in China's mobile payment industry. With the guidance of the PBoC, we inspired and bounced ideas off each other.

I remember one moment very clearly. After we had spent quite a lot of time discussing different security components and security requirements, a new question occurred to us: should all equipment be made with these components and to these requirements? For example, when we use a computer, we can transfer small amounts like ¥100 directly. But when you have a large amount of money to transfer, like ¥100,000, you have to use the bank's USB dongle. Both of these transfers are happening in a trusted environment, but the security levels are obviously different.

To address this question, the Huawei team proposed a scale of security capabilities. By defining the security level of smart devices, the scale could inform consumers of what financial transactions are safe for each level of security, and that would benefit the entire security key industry. This proposal was taken up by the working group.

Next, we had to work out the details of the scale, which took us five dedicated meetings. The debate was robust throughout, and the meetings got larger and larger as time went on, until we eventually ran out of chairs in our conference room. We ruefully realized that this was obviously a more controversial issue than we had thought. At the sixth meeting of the working group, we finally reached a consensus and produced a four-level scale that defined the degree of trusted payment environment supported by the mobile device. For each level, we defined the minimum set of security capabilities. A device would have to instantiate all of these capabilities in order to be given this rating; and for each rating, we defined what financial services the device could support.

In retrospect, those debates over the security scale were a reflection in miniature of the entire process. Developing a standard was a continual process of debate and argument, until we could finally reach an agreement. Many of the definitions included in the standard took many meetings to hammer out.

Before we started the approval phase, we had to assess the standard's feasibility and accuracy, and eliminate any potential risks from applying it market-wide. The PBoC appointed Huawei to lead the pilot programme, and we began working with test bodies to assess and certify the standard. The pilot programme was not just a test of our standard, but of Huawei's own products. Huawei phones that met the requirements of the standard were to be bombarded with innumerable attacks. They would have to survive attack after attack in order to prove that the standard we had designed was effective, and that the security key in Huawei phones was robust.

This was the first time anyone had ever carried out this kind of testing, so our testing partners had to design the test sample from scratch. The certifying partner had to record every issue, however small, arising during the process, which would be the raw input into their assessment. We were also there to shepherd the products through the tests, providing more than 100 design documents and description files. Our R&D staff sat in on the tests, and analysed each problem as it arose. After months of attacks, the first test report was ready. It found that Huawei had produced a secure product, and that the standard was feasible. This result meant that the whole industry could feel confident in building security keys into phones.

CCB takes the first step

The hardest part of any project is getting started. No one was willing to jump first and build a product before the PBoC had certified a working security standard, and before the industry had grown mature. It was going to be a big challenge to find a partner to work with us on the very first security key.

We spoke to the heads of several banks and found that everyone could technically recognize the value and potential of the security key. But everyone seemed to be in the wait-and-see phase when it came to the commercial use of the security key. As a result, our initial progress was slow. The excitement we had felt at completing the standard tests started to turn to anxiety and confusion. But it was just at this time that an opportunity arrived.

One August morning, we received a phone call from an executive at the China Construction Bank (CCB). He told us he was in a meeting with relevant directors of the CCB S branch, and he wanted us to tell them all about the new product. We had spoken to the CCB before, and he liked the product a lot. But we never realized that that meeting had planted the seed that would turn into our first partnership.

We got ourselves ready to meet the head of the S branch. In our meeting we explained the security key, how it worked, and what it would do. We were happy to see that the CCB had been closely following the latest developments in mobile finance. They had a lot of mobile financial customers, so our two companies made an excellent match. And we found that our ideas for innovation were well-aligned as well. The S branch not only liked the security key itself, they had their own ideas about how it could be used. It was designed to help individuals transfer large amounts securely, without the need for a second security device. But the CCB suggested that the security key could also help corporate bank customers generate their financial reports, reconcile their statements and complete other similar paperwork online. This would help the bank answer their corporate customers' demand for mobile payments. When we heard this, we clapped our hands. It was clear that the S branch was not just on the same page as us, but was bringing its own ideas to the table, and that our partnership would open up new avenues.

Very quickly, the S branch sent word that they were ready to begin a pilot programme with us, and that the bank's group leadership was very supportive of this new innovation. With that, our first security key programme was launched. Customers of the S branch who owned a Huawei phone with the new technology built in found themselves able to easily and securely make payments, transfer funds, pay utility bills, repay loans and complete many other financial operations.

The S branch was the first bank to try out Huawei's security key

Grand launch

On 20 October 2017, the HUAWEI Mate 10 was launched in Shanghai. Richard Yu, CEO of Huawei's Consumer BG, bounded onto the stage, and pulled out two Mate 10 phones from his jacket and trouser pockets. His first move was to show off the new camera functions. He then explained the features of the new phone, and he proudly announced that Huawei was the first phone maker to pass finance-level security assessments and tests. Leading industry partners – the CCB, Huishang Bank and Alipay – were the first financial institutions to offer their services through our certified security technology. Our team held their phones aloft to record the moment of the announcement. How many hours of work had gone into this moment? But now, it all felt worth it.

The security key shocked the financial industry in China. The media reported the innovation widely, and it went viral on social media. Shortly after the launch of the Mate 10, a dozen or more major banks called us to express their interest in working with Huawei and using the security key. Today, we are offering services for the CCB, Alipay, Huishang Bank and Jincheng Bank. Jinshang Bank and Bank of Nanjing are getting ready for the test and commercial deployment of the security key.

We are also very happy to see that the *Mobile Device Payment Trusted Environment Specification* has been officially released. This shows the level of recognition for us by China's most important financial regulator, and it has helped create the conditions for our products to be rolled out to the entire financial industry. It means that we can promote our security key to banks with greater confidence. And it is not just banks; third-party payment providers are carefully studying the standard. Huawei's work has given them new confidence and dynamism as well.

An increasing number of consumers are now using our security key to secure their mobile payments. The development of the security key was the result of the entire industry working together. We are confident that with the support of our partners, the invisible padlock that our security key places on our users' mobile wallets will keep their money safe for years to come.

12

Huawei Red in the Shadow of the Mountains of Heaven

By Zhu Zhenwei

In April 2014, I applied to leave my position in which I managed the sale of devices through telecom operators in the Greater China region. I was going to develop our direct-to-consumer sales in an exciting new territory: Xinjiang.

That year, I was 29 years old. Apparently, I was the youngest sales manager in Greater China. The saying goes that the young are bold and foolish, and I guess that was me. I wanted to make my mark, and I thought this was the way to do it. It was just selling phones, after all – how hard could it be? I would come to learn that selling directly to consumers is completely different from selling to operators. And in a massive, sparsely populated territory like Xinjiang, everything is twice as hard as you might imagine.

Who will get our phones to the consumers?

In 2014, 4G was being rolled out across China, and consumers were willing to spend more and more on good smartphones. All of the mobile phone brands were battling to win a place in the market. Huawei, which had always operated on a B2B basis in the past, was transitioning to the B2C domain.

Selling direct to consumers meant that we were no longer dealing with just one or two operator customers. It was no longer about getting orders from big customers, shipping them goods, and then sitting back and enjoying the results. Now we would have millions of individual consumers. We didn't know who they were, where they were or what they liked, but we had to win over each and every one. How were we to do it? How could we put a Huawei phone in the hands of every potential buyer?

Xinjiang makes up one sixth of China's total land area. But the total population across all of this vast space is only about the same as that of Shanghai. Huawei didn't have any retailer contacts in Xinjiang. We didn't have any of our own stores, and our sales team was just five people. Even worse, we had all come from operator network sales. No one had retail experience in the consumer market. But our team had to deal with 1.6 million square kilometres of sales territory. Clearly, we couldn't square this circle by just running around the retailers ourselves.

Fortunately, Greater China sales leadership gave us a solution: use a fulfilment distributor to get our phones out to many retail partners at the same time. That would get Huawei phones into the hands of consumers fast. But it was an entirely new area to us. How on earth could we find a fulfilment distributor?

We had to start somewhere, so first of all we just went knocking on doors. We split up, and visited all of the phone stores in Urumqi and the 16 other major towns in Xinjiang. What we discovered was that Xinjiang has a lot of phone stores, and the market is totally fragmented. They were all individually owned. With such a complex market, our established way of doing things was not going to work. Without a knowledgeable mentor to guide me, I felt lost. I didn't know what to do next. But I pulled together all of my resources, and scrambled the beginnings of a plan. We identified the biggest shopping areas in each of the towns and selected five retailers in each one.

Then we split up again, and began negotiations with each store owner. However, progress was very difficult. The first time we met with them, every store owner asked the same questions: "What's the wholesale price? What kind of in-store promotions are you going to provide? What rebates will you give us? What are the retail incentives?"

I felt like I was drowning in a sea of retail jargon. All of the retailers had all heard of Huawei, but none of them were particularly welcoming. They all thought that we were unproven in the retail market, and had no confidence in our ability to sell phones directly to consumers. After a few minutes, each conversation seemed to grind to a halt, and I was left red-faced. All I could do was go straight to the point, "Sir, how many phones can you buy? Can you tell us how many of our phones you can sell?"

The inevitable result was that we failed to gain any real partnership with the retailers.

Psychological games with a husband and wife team
After being given the cold shoulder by the retailers, I realized it was time to think again. We weren't great negotiators, at least not yet. So, was there a way to work around this weakness and focus instead on building retailers' confidence and interest in the Huawei brand?

After asking myself this question, I went to visit one of the big retailers in the town of Korla. When I got there, I found that the owners were a couple. I handed them my business card and explained what I wanted to talk to them about. The wife simply nodded, without saying a word. She kept her eyes down, wiped the table and served the tea. The husband sat down to talk to me. I started to tell them about Huawei's background and about our corporate culture. I told them about Huawei Consumer BG's plans for the future, and the selling points of our phones. I explained how we would help our customers make money ... We sat for three hours straight, and two-and-a-half hours of that was me talking. My hosts seemed entirely unimpressed. They didn't respond to anything I'd said, but they didn't turn me away, either.

At dinner time, the owners asked me to eat with them, more out of politeness than anything else. The husband sat in the host's chair, and his wife still said nothing. In order to break the embarrassing silence, I took out my phone and used it to demonstrate the functions. I explained to them how the HUAWEI Mate 7, soon to be launched, would be a high-quality phone, with a large screen, fingerprint recognition and long battery life. These were features that few phones then could match. The husband still said little in response to my presentation. I couldn't figure him out at all! After talking for another hour, my mouth was getting dry. All of a sudden, the wife spoke up for the first time, interrupting me: "Zhang, you come and sit here. I'll speak to Mr Zhu now." I suddenly realized what was going on: the real boss here was the wife. The husband was actually just an assistant.

She had been spending this time observing me, and once she started talking, everything was suddenly much easier. That retailer became our very first retail partner in Xinjiang, and is still one of our biggest retail partners in the region. Later, the boss explained to me that Huawei's consumer marketing at the time was very poor. What finally made the decision for her was the products themselves, and the commitment of the Huawei team. She saw that people from Huawei would work every conceivable angle to achieve their goals. And Huawei's phones certainly had a lot of potential. So, she decided to take a chance on us.

Selling direct to consumers meant that we were no longer dealing with just one or two operator customers … Now we would have millions of individual consumers … How were we to do it? How could we put a Huawei phone in the hands of every potential buyer?

Receiving training on a new product before the public launch

Even though we had finally got our first break, by the time the Mate 7 was launched in September 2014, we only had four retail partners. By October, the Mate 7 was a sensation. All of a sudden, the stores that had turned us away earlier were now calling us up, and our retail network began gradually expanding.

We also started building our retail sales skills so that we could cope with the new demand. It was not easy, but we learned from experience. For a period of six months or more, I took an average of 74 phone calls every day. All of my time was spent putting out fires. But gradually, we developed some effective practices for dealing with local retailers: during the days, we would visit the stores and help with sales, and set up Huawei experience stores in the key shopping districts. In the evenings, we would learn how to read sales data, start building processes, train our in-store promoters and learn sales techniques from our competitors and other major retail brands.

By the end of 2015, we had expanded our network in Xinjiang to 15 partners across the 16 prefectures, and we managed to double our 2014 sales. Finally, the Huawei flower was blossoming in Xinjiang.

Connecting the last mile

I had my first taste of success in the B2C market. Unfortunately, I got overconfident at that point. I started to believe that I had busted open the consumer market on my own. But when we held the Xinjiang year-end review meeting for 2015, one of the retail advisors for Ili Prefecture gave us some new food for thought.

An older man had taken a three-hour bus ride from a county town to the Huawei shop in Ili to ask about a problem with his phone. This gentleman had bought a Huawei phone in his local town, but he didn't know how to use many of its features. As a result, he thought that the phone didn't even have the functions that he wanted, and worried that the phone was actually broken.

Immediately, the room erupted. All of our sales staff had very similar issues. People in the small towns couldn't find Huawei stores, and there were no Huawei sales people to teach them how to use the phones. They weren't getting the Huawei services they needed.

We had missed a crucial element in our sales plan: our final customers were ordinary members of the public. Even if we could connect with the retailers, and put our phones in front of the consumers, we were not managing to deliver the Huawei experience that goes with the phone. The only thing to do was to start spending more time out in the small stores. We would have to get out into the territory, and get closer to our customers.

In the first half of 2016, the Greater China region launched a major new programme called the 'sowing seeds project.' By that time, the Xinjiang team had grown to about 40 staff. I put up a map of Xinjiang, and assigned everyone their tasks: there were 95 towns, with a combined population of 20 million. We were going to work out a detailed retailing plan in Xinjiang, and we were going to do it in the next two months!

We identified 88 key shopping districts where phones were sold. Everyone agreed on the strategy of showing the consumers what Huawei is. We would go to the county towns, which were not large, but were where the vast majority of people lived. Then we would make sure that every county town had at least one Huawei experience store, in an easy-to-find location. This was our 'last mile,' and would bridge the gap between Huawei and our customers.

In July, one of our distributors told us that a phone retailer in Aral, a town in Aksu, was interested in setting up the first county-level experience store. This sounded very promising, and I went straight there. The owner of the store was originally from Fujian, a coastal province on the other side of China. He had taken a trip back to Fujian to see his family, and liked the Huawei experience stores he had seen. However, he was worried that the consumers in this town in Xinjiang would not be willing to pay Huawei prices. I took him with me, and we conducted an on-the-spot survey. As each shopper entered the store, I asked them: "Have you heard of Huawei? Do you know the names of any Huawei phones?" I was pleased to find that everyone had heard of Huawei, and that everyone's perception of Huawei phones was that they were really good quality. Then I took the owner for a tour of local stores. There were a dozen stores in the town, but only one was selling a Huawei product, and that was an old phone from 2013. But this store owner told me that many of his local friends were using top-of-the-range phones.

We had a clear answer to our question: local consumers didn't lack the spending power; they didn't lack understanding of the Huawei brand; what they lacked was a place that could provide them with Huawei phones, and where they could receive better Huawei services and products.

Once he had seen this, the store owner started to feel the same confidence that I felt, and he decided to work with us to build a Huawei experience store. We set up a store following the same design that they use for Huawei stores all over the country, ensuring a consistent Huawei experience at every customer touchpoint: the same store front, the same signs, the same lightboxes, the same advertising … We helped them train in-store promoters, and gave them the same uniforms and the same service with a smile. Once we'd started, and word-of-mouth started to spread, more and more people started visiting, specifically to buy a Huawei phone. Huawei became a common sight in Xinjiang's county towns. By the end of 2017, we had set up more than 40 experience stores at county level. Huawei red was spreading across Xinjiang.

A Huawei experience store opens in Danlu, Urumqi

Localizing: hiring people who understand the customers

In the retail trade, they often talk in terms of three things: people, products and places. We now had the place, and our products were of high quality. The rest of our work would focus on people – the customers.

Every day we visited stores, and every month we had to do a shift in a store, meeting customers. We required every manager to do this, but when I visited the stores in Urumqi and Yining, I found there were still a lot of problems with the services being provided. For example, the Huawei sales promoters knew how to boast about the phone's features, but not how to explain what these features were good for, so the customers weren't getting the information they needed. Often, stores did not have a decent range of samples for customers to try, so the shopping experience was not interactive, experiential or participatory. Users who already owned Huawei products would come into stores to ask more questions about them, but they received very little attention and service. Very few stores stocked official Huawei accessories. Residents of other ethnicities often had difficulty talking to the store assistants, and Xinjiang has a lot of different ethnicities ...

Based on the problems we observed, we conducted surveys and spoke to the customers in stores to find out exactly what services were most important to them during the process of finding out about, buying and using their Huawei phones. We put the findings into effect in all our stores.

Hotan, in southern Xinjiang, is 95% Uighur, and most local business is done in the Uighur language. In addition, only 20% of locals also understand Chinese. The first time our sales representative in Hotan went to spend time in a local store, he saw a Uighur customer come in to learn about the features of Huawei phones.

Unfortunately, when the sales staff spoke to him in Chinese, he couldn't understand a word they were saying. The staff didn't speak the Uighur language, so the best they could do was draw pictures. The customer looked completely confused and left, disappointed.

We needed to stop language being a barrier. We needed people who understood the customers best to serve the customers. We placed recruitment ads in the local media in the Uighur language, put word out in the industry that we were hiring, walked around other stores, and much more. We used every method we could think of to hire Uighur sales staff. At first, progress was very slow. The language barrier slowed us down, and locals in Hotan didn't know much about Huawei. For at least a couple of weeks, we didn't see a single suitable candidate. In desperation, we asked local retailers for help. By working with locals already on the ground, we were finally able to locate some in-store promoters who were bilingual. To enhance our visual appeal to target customers, and so they could understand the phones more easily, we also asked our Uighur staff to help us redesign the stores. On our signs, counters and displays, we wanted to add Uighur, so that our customers could see and understand our products at a glance.

To prevent the problem of drowning customers in figures, we trained our sales promoters in marketing techniques. We ensured that they knew everything about our phones' features, specifications, processors and operating systems before they went out and started talking to the customers. I remember in October 2016, when the nova phone was launched. I watched a young customer, perhaps 30 years old, who said that he had seen a poster advertising the phone out in the town. He liked the camera functions and wanted to know more. Our Uighur salesperson replied to his questions fluently and expertly, and the customer looked very happy. In less than ten minutes, he had made his decision and purchased a phone.

Xinjiang has many different ethnic groups – 47 in total – and in the future we will be doing more to meet the needs of our customers in other ethnic groups. We will provide a tailored experience and services for them.

Xinjiang, in north-west China, is home to some of the most glorious scenery in the world. The Mountains of Heaven run east to west through the region. It boasts glaciers, lakes, grasslands, forests, ranches and rivers. To me it is beautiful but, until very recently, Xinjiang was like a desert for Huawei Consumer. Luckily, we are now established here, and although it has been hard, we have transformed the situation. We have learned what it means to be customer-centric. We have learned to give our customers a better class of service. Now, after years of hard work, wherever the shadows of the Mountains of Heaven fall, they fall on Huawei red.

13

The Huawei Spirit Is Alive in Huawei Partners

By Yang Xinrui, Danimar Cohelho, Yang Xin and Cagdas Sendur

In Huawei's Consumer BG, the frontline customer service team includes service store workers and hotline operators, as well as customer service representatives on the Huawei website. These people are closest to our customers, always there to answer customer queries, help them buy phones and provide after-sales services. There are 8,000 people in this team, working around the world. Most of them are actually employed by Huawei's partners. Nevertheless, every one of them lives by Huawei's philosophy of customer service – striving to make every service a positive memory for our customers.

Even the hard-of-hearing can hear how hard we work
(Yang Xinrui, Technical Adviser at the Huawei Customer Service Centre in Harbin, China)

I'm a technical adviser at Huawei's Customer Service Centre in Harbin, China. My job is to fix Huawei devices if something goes wrong.

One day, I received a HUAWEI P8 smartphone. The customer reported that sometimes no sound was coming through the earphones when he was trying to listen to music or talk on the phone. I tested the phone for 20 minutes, but it seemed to be functioning fine. I walked out of the repair room to ask the customer some questions about the details of the fault. The moment I saw our customer, Mr Lian, I instantly understood how important it was for us to fix the fault.

Yang Xinrui repairing a phone

Mr Lian was wearing a hearing aid, and he had to talk to me through his wife. I completely understood how Mr Lian must have felt, as one of my uncles also suffered from hearing impairment. Because of his hearing aid, my uncle could not hold the phone up to his face to talk, and instead must use his earphones. Sound is both wonderful and precious to my uncle. Therefore, I told myself that I must do everything I could to fix this phone, and that I would succeed as long as I tried hard enough.

I asked Mr Lian to leave the phone at the Customer Service Centre, and told him that we would let him know when it was ready to pick up. After numerous tests, I finally found the cause of the problem at about 10 am the next day. There was a fault with a small circuit board that was supporting the headset jack. I was thrilled to have found the problem. Once I replaced the faulty board, the phone was once again in perfect working order.

I knew that Mr Lian's home was a four-hour drive from the Customer Service Centre, which was a long trip for him. So I wanted to make sure that the fault would not occur again. I tested the phone over and over, playing music and making phone calls until I was absolutely sure that the problem was fixed.

On the third day, I called Mr Lian's wife and told her the phone was ready for pickup. She said they were in a hurry and would need to leave immediately after collecting the phone. To save them some time, I told her that I would clear the phone's memory of all the music I had played and all the phone calls I had made, so that they could just pick up the phone and go. However, she asked me to leave the data on the phone, as they wanted to know what tests I had performed.

On the fifth day after Mr Lian had picked up his phone, a package was delivered to our Customer Service Centre. It contained a red banner saying thank you, along with a thank-you letter. According to the letter, Mr Lian had found the records of the hundreds of songs I had played and the dozens of phone calls I had made during testing. He had been deeply moved by the effort that I had put into this small repair job.

It was just another ordinary day at work for me. When Huawei provides services for our customers, our key commitment is: always approach a customer's problem with a positive attitude, and fix it fast. We must put ourselves into our customers' shoes, so that we understand how important it is to fix their problems. Our customers should always have a pleasant service experience, even if we are just replacing the tiniest electronic component.

Three visits make a Huawei fan for life
(Danimar Coelho, Manager of the Huawei Customer Service Centre in Madrid, Spain)

It was a normal Saturday, just 20 minutes before closing time, when a customer rushed to the Customer Service Centre looking very anxious. I quickly walked over to see what I could do for her.

Her name was Maria, and she told me she had just flown from the island of Mallorca to Madrid. Unfortunately, she had lost her Huawei phone on the way, and would be spending a week in Madrid on business. She nervously said, "I have no way of accessing my contacts or my emails." I completely understood her anxiety, got her a glass of water and listened to all she had to say. I then taught Maria how to recover her contact list and emails via her email account. Before she left, I suggested that she report the loss to the police, and told her that she could come back to me if she had any other problems.

The next Monday morning, Maria returned to the Customer Service Centre. Her friend had lent her a mobile phone, which wasn't made by Huawei, and she wanted me to help her transfer her contacts onto this phone and configure the settings. This was a lot of work, and she wasn't even using a Huawei phone. Still, I agreed to help her, because she seemed to trust me.

The first thing she needed was a SIM card, which she had to request from the network operator. I helped her find the right address, and then she went to get the new SIM card. Maria returned one hour later, and I helped her recover her contacts.

The team at the Huawei Customer Service Centre in Madrid

A few days later, about 5 pm, Maria came to the Customer Service Centre for the third time. She was returning to Mallorca that day, so she came to say goodbye to me and wanted to buy a new Huawei phone from us. This made me very happy, because her visit meant she trusted me. However, we didn't sell phones at the Customer Service Centre. Therefore, I told her how to get to the nearest Huawei retail store, and Maria eventually went home with a new HUAWEI P9. She said to me, "You guys left me with good memories of my trip to Madrid. Thank you very much for your excellent service. This experience has left me liking the Huawei brand even more."

If consumers feel warmth and a human connection when receiving services from Huawei, the Huawei brand will grow through word-of-mouth, and we can reach even more people. In my opinion, after-sales service is not simply about fixing devices; more importantly, it is about connecting with consumers. We must always be ready to do our very best with every customer. This is the principle that I work by.

If consumers feel warmth and a human connection when receiving services from Huawei, the Huawei brand will grow through word-of-mouth, and we can reach even more people … We must always be ready to do our very best with every customer.

One extra question turns a complaint into a thank you

(Yang Xin, Hotline Operator and Quality Inspection Specialist at the Huawei Consumer Contact Centre in Shanghai, China)

I have worked at Huawei's Consumer Contact Centre in Shanghai for two years, where I was a hotline operator for one and a half years. I am now a quality inspection specialist. Working on the front lines can be very difficult, especially when customers come to us with complaints. Customers are often unhappy or upset when they come to us, so we must be positive during every interaction we have with them. We firmly believe that every interaction with a customer is an opportunity to convey our warmth and a human touch to them.

Last June, I received a call from a Mr Cao in Beijing, who had just bought a Huawei phone for the first time. To his dismay, the box the phone came in did not contain a user manual. He thought he had made a poor choice, and that we weren't respecting the needs of senior citizens. I patiently listened to him and calmed him down. Then I explained to him that the user manual contains too much information to be useful to most people. I told him that instead, we provide a quick start-up guide in the box, and users can access the full manual using an app on their phone, or download the manual from the Huawei website. However, Mr Cao still wasn't happy, and insisted on making a formal complaint.

Our normal approach to this kind of situation is to take down the customer's request, and escalate the issue to the department that handles complaints. But customer issues do not come out of thin air, so I decided to ask him one more question: "What did you need the user manual for?"

It turned out that he was having a problem using his phone: he did not know how to upload photos from his phone to a computer. Over the phone, I taught him how to do this, step by step. Mr Cao was not very practised with a phone, and this process took nearly three hours.

The way I see it, when a customer complains, we shouldn't take it personally. They are not making a complaint about us; they are just unhappy with a product or a service. That's why I like to ask our customers a few extra questions to try to understand what they really need and find out what they really want to say.

Ultimately, Mr Cao withdrew the complaint, and praised us for our service. I still remember what he said to me: "Your service represents the Huawei brand. If you keep providing excellent services like this, Huawei will go from strength to strength." He inspired me to keep doing my best for our customers.

I also realized something else: many customers seek help not because there is a problem with the product; they just don't know how to use the product. Therefore, part of our job is to help our customers easily understand and use Huawei products. In fact, this is a hugely important part of the services provided by the Consumer BG.

I have now transitioned from hotline operator to quality inspection specialist, and I shoulder more responsibility than before. It hasn't always been easy. There were times when I was blamed and ended up in tears. There were even times when I considered leaving because the job was just too stressful. However, I always put those experiences out of my mind when I consider the appreciation and encouragement that customers give me.

I focus all of my attention on being the best quality inspector that I can be. I carefully listen to the recordings of my colleagues, so that I can identify any problems and help them give the best possible Huawei service to every customer.

Workers receiving new product training

One hour: enough to gain a brand ambassador

(Cagdas Sendur, Manager of the Huawei Customer Service Centre in Amsterdam, the Netherlands)

On 11 October 2017, a lady in her early 60s entered Huawei's Customer Service Centre in Amsterdam. She seemed a little shy, and I went over to ask her what I could do for her.

She told me that she had just bought a HUAWEI P10, based on her friend's recommendation, but that she did not know how to use it. After seeing the Huawei logo on our Customer Service Centre, she thought we might be able to help, so she came in. She was worried that she may not be welcome because she hadn't come to get her phone fixed. But as far as we are concerned, every customer is welcome. I assured the lady that I would try my best to help her and got her a cup of coffee to help her relax.

After carefully listening to all she had to say, I learned that she was most concerned about how to copy the data from her old phone to the new phone. I helped her adjust the necessary settings on the phone, and copied all her data over using Huawei's unique phone clone function.

The lady was incredibly happy to learn that data replication could be so easy. I also spent some time showing her how to use some of the phone's most commonly used functions, and encouraged her to learn more about these features to get the most out of them. By this time a small queue had formed behind the lady, and my colleagues were all busy serving other customers. The lady was embarrassed by this and said to the people behind her, "Sorry for keeping you waiting. You can go before me. I can wait." There was some muttering in the queue, but the lady and I both found it heart-warming to see that most of the customers didn't mind. The customer right behind her smiled and said, "That's OK. We can wait for our turn."

This taught me a valuable lesson. When we provide one customer with the best services possible, other customers see it. This makes them realize that they will also receive the most high-quality service.

Huawei's Customer Service Centre in Amsterdam

I spent around 70 minutes helping the lady to better understand her new phone. She was very grateful for what I did, and said she would let everyone know about the unforgettable service she had received at Huawei's Customer Service Centre. She told me that she would become a brand ambassador for Huawei.

We need to seize every opportunity to make it easier for customers to use Huawei products. Sometimes, it takes just an hour to make our customers happy and satisfied. I only took an hour to gain a brand ambassador, and I think that's priceless.

More growth, more good memories

Heart-warming stories like these play out every day. However, we are keenly aware that not every customer receives a good service experience. This is something we never want to see. We must continue reflecting on what we do well, and what needs improving. This will allow us to improve the services we deliver on an ongoing basis.

Huawei has grown rapidly in the consumer sector over the past few years, and so has our service network. However, there are still areas for us to improve in terms of geographical coverage and user experience. In particular, our service centres and online service platforms are struggling to keep pace with the growth of our business. Our next step will be to expand our network of service stores and develop self-service capabilities. In addition, we should focus more on service management in order to deliver standardized services and develop strong support capabilities.

Every service employee in the Consumer BG is committed, heart and soul, to customer service. We believe that our customers can feel the warmth of a human connection in every service we deliver, ensuring every Huawei service experience will be a happy memory.

No Roads to Follow

By Zhu Ping

In March 2014, I joined the Huawei Consumer team and took charge of sales in China. I had over a dozen years of experience in information and communications technology networks. I had been a product manager and a customer manager. I had spent time as a manager in China, overseas and serving multinational telecom operators. But selling consumer electronics was new to me. The four years since then have passed in the blink of an eye. The consumer jungle has no pre-existing roads to follow, but we have blazed our own trail. Along the way we have encountered thickets of complexity and numerous frustrations. But ultimately we were able to overcome all these difficulties and I have been inspired by the successes that unity and hard work have brought us.

Data from third-party market research firms tells us that Huawei became the most desired phone brand in China in 2017, and in 2018 we continued our steady rise. People ask me, how did you manage to do this? I believe that it is the result of our commitment to customers, our commitment to brand and quality, and our unstinting investments of money and effort.

Strategic transformation: the turn to consumers
A necessary change in thinking

In 2014, major telecom operators in China were investing their money in the evolution to 4G networks. They had little left over to subsidize contract phones. At the same time, the internet was providing a new model for marketing phones, and the established phone makers were struggling to adapt. Consumers were willing to spend more on their phones, but they were spending rationally, and they had high expectations of quality.

The 'battlefield' had changed, tactics had changed, the tools had changed, the players had changed and the users had changed. How were we to adapt?

Back at the end of 2011, Huawei had named consumer business one of our core lines of business. In 2012, we introduced four major new lines of phone: the D/Mate, P, G and Y. We had set our sights on the mid-range and high-end phone market, but we had not yet succeeded in establishing ourselves firmly as a major player. In the first half of 2014, the company leadership and Huawei Consumer CEO,

Richard Yu, joined us to make a number of visits to our field offices and quickly came to a decision: this period of upheaval was our opportunity to get out in front of our competitors. We were to commit ourselves fully to a consumer-oriented strategy, and invest heavily to help it to succeed. This would enable us to build a solid consumer-facing organization with all the capabilities we needed.

At that point, I had been in my new position for just three months, and I didn't yet feel that I had enough credibility to start throwing my weight around. I was in listen, watch and discuss mode: listen attentively to users and experts; watch our partners and competitors, see what different business scenarios were like; and discuss with the team, brainstorm and develop solutions.

At that time, for a number of reasons, Huawei did not have a strong team that could engage with our channel partners and retailers. Our processes, IT systems and data handling were all outdated, so we could not even obtain a clear picture of purchases, sales and inventory. And we had just started building the team and skills that we would need to manage the customer experience. We had hired many people with experience in this area, but they were still integrating into the team.

Everything is hardest at the beginning: it was a process of changing the way we thought, and absorbing the fuel we would need as we carved our own pathway to success in the B2C world.

The Mate 7 was a must-win

Soon after I arrived, we prepared to launch the Mate 7. We all knew that this would be a critical test, as it was an opportunity for us to get ahead of our competitors in the consumer market. For me and my team it was do-or-die. The success or failure of a flagship phone can have a huge impact on the brand it represents. As we prepared for the Mate 7, I decided to show the team how important it was: "If we don't hit our targets with this phone, I will be stepping down from my position."

The phone market is a jungle. It combines all of the most challenging aspects of consumer sales in one place. First, we were faced with many different competitors and partners. The industry was changing fast, and technology and the ability to work at a global level became new drivers of transformation. Second, the market is made up of a vast number of individual consumers and the demand for customization is high. With over one billion users to serve, continuously moving and adapting without good approaches was a frightening possibility. Mobile internet and social media were also growing at a dramatic pace, and were transforming consumer habits and behaviour. Buyers now wanted more services and more interaction, and they wanted a trust-based relationship with their brands. Our retail partners, both online and offline, also needed to provide great breadth and depth of coverage, and a positive retail environment. If we were to survive and find our way through this jungle, we would have to find our own direction and our own approach. Choosing the right strategy was critical.

The Mate 7 was the third phone in the Mate series. During the product planning phase, we conducted a survey involving over 40,000 Huawei customers, and decided to make business users our target market. They reported that they wanted a big screen, long battery life and security, and on that basis we incorporated new features into our EMUI operating system. We also included a big battery, fingerprint scanner, a high screen-to-body ratio and a metal body.

The phone itself was a one. But our brand, services, marketing, channels, supply chain and ecosystem were all zeros. The product was the core factor, of course, but if all those other zeros could not be dragged up, then we would never be able to realize the value of that factor. We had many rounds of discussion on the right sales strategy for the Mate 7, and we eventually worked out a plan: we should stick to our guns when targeting the high-end market. The price should be at least ¥3,500, and we should plan to sell more than one million units.

However, this plan was not met with total agreement. "No Chinese phone has ever sold as much as that."

"The last two generations of the Mate didn't sell well at all – can we really move that many?"

"The buyers love foreign phone brands, and we don't have much experience in brand marketing. Can Huawei really change the way consumers think?"

But we were confident that the Mate 7 was Huawei's opportunity to break into the high-end market. It was the right phone, with the right features. All we had to do was market it properly, and we knew that we had a potential winner on our hands. At the time, we did not have much budget for marketing in China, so we couldn't pay for a marketing push ourselves. We had to borrow money from HQ as an investment in the brand. We also took a gamble in the marketing strategy, following an innovative approach that focused on deep data analysis, assessing market signals and the preferences of users, then combining our brand messaging and product features with the value that our users sought. We then exploited social marketing and word-of-mouth marketing channels for a full-spectrum marketing push. We also changed the way we approached retail, coordinating and balancing our online and offline sales so that we could get closer to the customers.

We held regular meetings with our core retail partners

In the end, the Mate 7 was a success – you couldn't get a Mate 7 for asking. It gave a massive boost to the Huawei brand, and freed our hands in the pricing of future phones. It also gave us the confidence that we could even win in the high-end phone market. And the success of the phone helped to define what would become the DNA of the Mate series: a big screen, long battery life, high performance and high security. Every subsequent Mate has been an exercise in continuing and refining that core DNA.

Execution of strategy: coordinating teams, channels and people

New organization for consumer focus, agility and shared vision

In the second half of 2014, HQ gave the China consumer product sales team more freedom to operate independently. We would be taking our lives into our own hands. The team adopted the four Ps of marketing: product, price, place and promotion. We reorganized so that we could better coordinate all of our teams that were working with different channel partners, break down barriers and get our team assigned in the most efficient way. We set up systems for product go-to-market, marketing, sales and services, then devolved responsibility for sales down to the province teams, then the city teams and even the county teams. They would have autonomy over how they operate. We built up stable teams in all of our more than 300 cities and territories across China, and encouraged everyone to offer our users the very best services and to win the sales we needed.

Working in the consumer market is like selling fresh seafood: you have to be swift and deft. That means you have to have your strategy right from the get-go, and there cannot be systems failures. At the country level, we made sure that our go-to-market, marketing, procurement, services and internal control/anti-corruption systems all had committees working efficiently to oversee them. We set a timetable with regular meetings every Monday to keep everyone on the same page, with the option to call same-day meetings for urgent issues. Speed was of the essence. The weekly sales meetings brought together all of the sales managers in the Desert Orchid meeting room, with the province managers phoning in to take part remotely. Our principle was that everyone had to be fully informed: not just about what was happening, but why it was happening as well. We made sure that everyone knew how to execute our policies and, more importantly, everyone had the same big-picture vision. In this way, we broke down any barriers to communication between teams or departments, and made our organization much more agile and efficient.

Some people did not understand what we were doing. For example, they thought that marketing decisions could simply be made by the marketing team. But we had to think about the fact that our market changed every day. The go-to-market process, user needs, plans and delivery, partner recommendations – all of these were in dynamic flux. If the marketing team just followed the original plan, and did not adapt dynamically to change, then they might fall out of step with the sales and services teams. To make sure that didn't happen, we set up the marketing committee. In the go-to-market committee, every major decision we made was based on the inputs and ideas from every member. Wherever possible, we aimed for unanimity. It was a process of debate, communication and coordination, and it helped to ensure that no individual errors of judgement or material risks slipped through the net. In the run up to the product launch, and in fact all the way through the product's lifecycle, we never said for sure that we could hit our targets.

At every moment, our priority was to steady the ship, maintain the pace, improve execution, anticipate upcoming problems, make decisions in good time and always choose the optimal pathway. In these past few years, we have run launch campaigns for many new phones. The blueprint for all of them came out of that Desert Orchid meeting room.

The long view: distribution channels and retail networks take time

We were pivoting to a new focus on selling directly to consumers. To succeed, we would need to build our own channels to market, and build them quick. Following the success of the Mate 7, Huawei started to get some recognition from channel partners. Many more companies wanted to talk to us. In fact, some came knocking on our door, with offers of free slots in over 1,000 outlets.

As the saying goes: always look beyond the horizon! We realized that working through the conventional distributors would ensure a foundation for healthy business operations, but we also needed to keep expanding the market in unconventional ways. We needed a healthy retail strategy. If a retailer wasn't confident about partnering with us, we would talk to them about Huawei's values, long-term strategy, and strong R&D. We would explain how we focus on our users, and aim to be the best in everything we do. When a retailer approached us, we also had to be willing to say no to those who weren't a good fit.

A retail network is not like a desk drawer, to be opened and shut any time you want. When a product is selling well, it's easy enough to open a new store. But if a store is not well-run, what happens? You lose not just the store, but your customers, and partners lose confidence in your brand. The retail team therefore set minimum standards to be met and a process to be followed before opening a new outlet. This kind of specialist work needs to be handled by retail specialists, so we also set a rule that we would only work with retailers who had successful track records. We also applied a survival-of-the-fittest approach, closing down any stores that did not meet our standards.

To ensure that our distribution channels were flowing smoothly, we needed transparent data. We set up a B2C digitization team, who would be in charge of developing our very first distribution data systems, so that our operations could be properly data-driven. In 2015, the purchase, sales and inventory system went online. It combined Huawei data with data from our distributors and retailers, supporting intelligent consumer-facing operations.

Today, the China sales team has 28 of its own IT systems, managing products, marketing, contracts, retail, services and suppliers. They support our business processes end-to-end, and are constantly being optimized. Many managers have been through a steep learning curve with data, from the random juggling of numbers to clear-headed analytics. As a result, efficiency has soared and risks are well-controlled. All of our team members have now learned to use the language of data to regulate their operations, and to deliver a good experience to our users and our partners.

Diverse team, shared vision
"Huawei does not have any natural resources to depend upon. What we do have is the brainpower of our employees. This is our oil, our forests and our coal. Human ingenuity is the creator of all wealth." Everything we do depends on people, whether it's an organizational restructuring, developing a business process, marketing or just implementing the strategy. Hardworking, talented people are not just the source of value creation in the company, they are also the foundation for the company's consumer-centricity strategy.

We attracted people from all sources. We also encouraged managers to move around, from city to city, province to province, and business domain to business domain, even from China to overseas. We brought in seasoned experts from our own industry and others, so that the team had the right mix of experience, expertise and creativity for the work that we had to achieve. It was a blend of people we poached from other Huawei departments, our own fast-track managers, experienced industry hires and entry-level graduates. Every single person benchmarked themselves against the best performers in the world, and focused on providing the best possible user experience and coordinating to maximize our effectiveness.

But it is never easy to bring together a group of disparate people and form them into a tight team. We created an environment that was focused and free from office politics. By effectively using both material and motivational incentives, we tried to prevent the seeds of greed and corruption from taking root, and to build a team that was full of dynamism. We wanted everyone to love the brand and fight for it. Managers were required to put Huawei's core values into practice, and to spend time out in the field, listening to the voices of our customers, our partners and our own people, and make improvements accordingly.

A staff badminton game

Strategic patience: winning the future with big services and new retail

A brand that represents both technology and beauty

In the China team, we stay true to our aspirations, and that means finding out what every group needs. We used to be organized by product, but we have now developed into a customer-oriented organization. The product series under the Huawei brand target different consumer groups: the Mate series is for high-end business users; the P series is for the high-end fashion-conscious market; the nova series for younger users, with its trendy look and cutting-edge technology.

Everyone knows that Huawei is a technology powerhouse, with the capacity to research and develop exciting new technologies. But not everyone realizes that Huawei also sets very high standards in terms of product design and aesthetics. The company has design centres in France, the UK, Germany, Sweden, Japan and Canada. Most importantly, we have our Aesthetics Research Centre in Paris. We always aim to combine the latest technology with a sense of artistry, so that our customers can directly perceive the beauty of technology.

Over the last few years, we have focused on the high-end market, and expanded our range of partners in other industries. For example, we sponsored China's top Go league to reinforce the 'intelligent' aspect of our brand. The Mate 10 was the first phone to introduce an AI chip, making us a leader in the new arena of phone engagement with the user. In our marketing efforts, we followed what our customers were thinking, which led us to develop our 'firefighter' advertisement for our smartphone's water-resistant function, widely praised for its emotional appeal. As an online-offline marketing campaign, "Take love home" made smart use of the reach of e-commerce to carry an emotional connection with the Huawei brand to wherever our customers are.

Big services, new retail

This is an era of competition over details. Services are one of the key aspects of creating a brand. They are an essential pillar in our business operations. Every sale is an opportunity to deliver services. Every experience is a service – this is the underlying concept of 'Big Services.' Over the last few years, Huawei has continuously striven to deliver better big services.

Today, the China sales team has built a complete sales and services network, covering every city and county. It includes nearly 1,000 Huawei-branded service outlets spread across the cities and key sales territories. In 2014, we introduced online customer services, including online sales, as a way for a call centre team to provide customized services. In 2018, the call centre had over 3,000 people, and handled more than 40 million tickets per year. The lines are open 24/7, and we ensure we answer more than 95% of calls we receive. We also made the first Friday, Saturday and Sunday of the month special service days. On these days, we serviced and cleaned phones and applied screen protectors for consumers for free. When the phones' warranty expired, we couldn't offer the services for free, but we did not charge anything for our own labour. We also launched a Battery Replacement programme, through which we would replace a phone's battery for just ¥99 even after the warranty expired.

Users just had to call our service location in advance, or they could courier the phone to us.

As well as our own locations, there are more than 3,000 authorized dealers, who can be found scattered throughout China's cities and 1,700 counties and regions. These outlets offer displays, sales, product experiences and responses to common questions. They are our interface with the customers and the foundation of our brand. Huawei also spent a lot of its own money dealing with copycat brands that aimed to deceive customers and could have harmed our own brand image.

The Huawei Intelligent Lifestyle showroom in Taiyuan

In April 2018, Huawei's first Intelligent Lifestyle showroom opened in Taiyuan, to be a place where we could share our vision of better lifestyles with our customers. It presents a series of lifestyle experiences in a simple, clean environment, so that customers can develop a multisensory, interactive understanding of the products. They can experience life in the fast lane or pursue a more easy-going life style.

Here, on an electronic screen, customers can tap the icons of the apps they would like to learn more about. They can also place orders online or chat to an experience consultant. All products are linked to the HiLink smart home platform, so that customers can experience how easy it is to take photos on their phone, and then use them to control other devices in the smart home ecosystem. On the online platform, customers can see activity notices in real time, browse new products or sign up for Huawei classes. In the store, the screen, which is nearly 30 square metres, along with the broad experience tables, offer a perfect example of what it means to be face-to-face with an interactive environment. The available content includes a smart assistant, the app store, a browser, Huawei music, Huawei video, Huawei Pay, Skytone and cloud storage. Each one is designed to maximize the value of the cloud for users.

Speaking with retail staff

The Huawei device product range now includes computers, tablets, wearables, smart speakers and routers that can be used for offices, sports, smart homes or cars. In our smart home ecosystem, we also offer selected partner products, so that customers can choose from a broad but high-quality range. In the coming 2019, Huawei will be opening more lifestyle experience centres in China's large cities, and setting benchmarks in terms of brand, experience and service.

Being customer-centric is a quest that never ends. We are runners in a long race, learning new things all the time, "absorbing the energy of the universe," working hard with our partners along the value chain, and using the best technology and services to create greater value and bring more fun to our customers.

15

The Phone Fortune-Tellers

By Gu Zhengdong

If you drop your phone on the floor, will it break? If you walk into a signal dead zone, will your call drop? If you turn your music up too loud, will you get distortion from your speakers?

In the past, the only way to answer these questions was to test, test and test. In 2014, as part of our quality control for the HUAWEI Mate 7 smartphone, we carried out drop tests on our models over and over again. Every time, ten phones were dropped from a height of one metre onto a granite surface, then we checked the phones for damage, updated our designs, cut new moulds and launched the next round of testing. The whole process took two to three months, and we smashed hundreds of phones before we found a form factor that met the reliability requirements.

It was a long, exhausting process. More importantly, it was an entirely reactive process. It wasted time, and increased our development costs. Could there be a better way to find design flaws? Could we know in advance what kind of design would make the phone break easily when dropped or why exactly it would break? What kinds of changes would increase its strength?

This is not just pie-in-the-sky dreaming. There is an answer to all of these questions, and it can be summed up in one word: simulation.

What is simulation? In simple terms, it is computer modelling. For example, when a phone is dropped from one metre high, everything happens very fast. With the naked eye, you cannot see exactly what happens during the fall, so it is hard to know why the phone broke. In a simulation, a virtual model is constructed on the computer based on the engineering drawings for the product. This model can then be used to simulate the process of dropping the phone, and the program can calculate exactly which components come under the most stress, and are most likely to break. This gives the engineers a lead on where they should be looking to improve the strength of the design.

This ability to predict the fortune of a phone can eliminate the need to carry out repeated testing. But in order for this 'phone fortune-teller' to be effective, it must be highly accurate. The virtual simulation results it produces must be exactly the same as what we get in real life. It also needs to be fast, if it is to be any use to our developers.

After the nightmare of having to smash hundreds of models of the Mate 7, I was determined to give Huawei a more powerful simulation engine. So I set a target for the structural simulation team:

improve simulation accuracy to 90%, and reduce simulation run time from a week to one day. When I announced this target, everyone was incredulous.

"That's ... not possible. No one in the world could create a simulation at that level."

"If we can't manage it within one year, then get it done in two," I replied. "If you can't do it in two years, then get it done in three. I don't care how you do it, we just need to get it done!"

This same goal was set not just for the structural simulators, but also for the antenna simulation team, the voice frequency team, the heat engineering team and the optical engineering team. All simulations had to improve! With that, everyone got to work trying to boost the performance of our simulation engines.

Many hands make light work

To achieve our targets, we would need some help. We needed to hire a team of real simulation experts.

During the 2014 graduate recruitment season, I visited Zhejiang University to find PhDs with the right kind of experience. Huawei was not yet a big name in mobile phones back then, so the response was rather underwhelming. I talked up a storm, describing what we do for more than an hour, and at the end issued my invitation: "So who is up for this simulation challenge? Raise your hand if you're interested!" The room was completely silent, and not a single hand went up. It was very awkward.

I continued my pitch: "Huawei is a very ambitious company. We're not simply trying to simulate what happens when you drop a phone from one metre high. We are trying to automate the entire phone engineering process! Simulation is a field with massive potential, and we very much hope that you will come and reach for these impossible goals with us."

Perhaps moved by my desperation more than anything else, two new PhDs did stay. From that day on, we started to get more and more talented people to join Huawei. Today, nearly half of our simulation team are PhDs.

Once we had this high-powered team we got to work, dealing with three major challenges: one, developing highly accurate and highly automated simulation algorithms; two, calculating the exact levels of stress, humidity and heat that would cause a fault for each component; and three, researching the properties of each component and material.

Internally, we formed a project team with top experts in our 2012 Labs and our overseas Centres of Expertise. Externally, we set up research partnerships with some of the top universities in Europe and North America. For example, we worked with some of the world's top labs to research various materials used in our devices and determine their stress characteristics under high-speed deformation or impact. This enabled us to build the most advanced database in the industry on dynamic material properties.

In terms of hardware, we made some bold investments. For our structural simulations, we created a high precision static environment and a dynamic material fatigue environment, to enable us to model the performance of materials over their entire lifetime. For antenna simulations, we created the world's highest-precision darkroom, and tested the performance characteristics of our antennas to unprecedented levels of precision. For electromagnetic fields, we measured the Earth's magnetic field, then created a Helmholtz coil with a diameter of just 1.1 mm, within which we could control the strength of the magnetic field with perfect precision. For heat flow, we developed a heat simulation system that could be applied to any circumstances and material, accurate down to the millisecond level.

This is the way Huawei does it: once we realize that a technology is going to be valuable for consumers, we spare no expense to get that technology right. We buy the best resources and hire the best people to make it happen.

The Huawei consumer simulation team

"Wow! Simulations can actually get the job done!"

By 2016, we had achieved a breakthrough in our simulations. Our structural simulation engine had achieved an industry-leading level of 90% accuracy. This meant that our simulations were now effectively a crystal ball in which we could see the future of our phones. They could predict potential design problems and offer solutions.

The simulation team

But just making these claims was no use. How could we demonstrate our new capabilities?

I remember the testing process for one of the Mate phones. After the phone was dropped, the dual cameras could no longer focus. Eight out of every ten phones came out blurry. We opened up the phones to take a look, and found that the spring plates had split on the motors that controlled the lens, leaving the lens angled slightly. As a result, the camera could not focus properly. With one lens, if the optical axis was askew, the phone could still focus. But with dual lenses, this was a problem: the two lenses needed to focus on the same object at the same time, so they had to be aligned to less than 0.1 mm.

The Quality Department and the lens manufacturer got together to discuss how to solve the problem many times, and in the end, the manufacturer almost gave up in frustration.

"It can't be done! If you're going to drop them from this height, the spring plates are going to break! It would be a miracle if they didn't."

We were stuck. If we couldn't solve this problem, then our dream of a dual-lens camera might be doomed to failure. And this was going to be one of our biggest selling points. If we couldn't make the two-lens camera work, then the phone would be considerably less attractive to our buyers. I couldn't bear to see such a brilliant design concept go to waste. I took a breath and said, "The simulation team will solve it!"

Once I'd said it, I had to make good on my promise. We created virtual camera units, including everything on the engineering drawings, at an incredible level of detail. Even the 40 µm-thick edge of the spring plate could be seen with absolute clarity. We next used a computer to model the entire drop test process, the simulation software applying physical dynamic formulas to determine the stresses on each component at the moment of impact. In the animation we produced, the 0.1 seconds of impact could be stretched out to any length we wanted. Just like watching a movie, we could go through it frame by frame, observing the changes in every component as they were stressed in different positions.

The stressed areas showed up in the animation in different colours – red when the stress exceeded danger levels – so the whole thing looked like one of those moving weather maps. The simulation found us our answer: the point at which the spring plate bends flashed up red, meaning it was overstressed. But if we just changed the shape and the angle of the corner of the plate, then the force could be distributed in a different way, and the camera would not break even when dropped. Very quickly, we were able to deliver a precise solution to the problem, and prove that it worked in real-life tests.

The entire process went like clockwork. When the structural engineers saw that we had a straightforward solution to the problem that had frustrated them for two months, they were stunned.

"Wow!" they said. "Simulations can actually get the job done!"

How to stop your screen eating your signal

Huawei phones have excellent connection quality, and the main reason for this is our high-performing antennas. However, antennas are also highly sensitive. Even just tweaking a single part of the circuit board or the phone shell can dramatically weaken signal reception. That's where simulations come into play more often.

Huawei's FullView Display screens are a lot of fun to use, but they caused a big problem for the antennas. The screen's indium tin oxide layer and flexible printed circuit encroach on the antenna clearance area, so an antenna that provided excellent connections suddenly had half of its signal eaten up by the screen.

Does good connection really have to be sacrificed for a FullView Display screen experience? The antenna engineers were not going to accept that. It was time to see if the simulation team could work its magic once again!

The antenna simulation team gradually got to grips with the task, and worked out how to create a model of the screen. The screen is a phone's largest component, simple from the outside, but with a whole world of complexity inside. Both the capacitive touch layer and the display layer have complicated wiring, but the wires are only a few micrometres in width and just a few hundred nanometres in thickness. The idea of creating an accurate model of the current's flow across this complex and delicate system seemed beyond our grasp.

But if we could not model the entire thing in one go, could we break it down into sections? We decided to develop equivalent-circuit models, where we would break the screen down into five separate elements – the glass pane, the touch layer, the display layer and so on – and model each one separately. Then we could combine the models to try to reproduce the overall effect on the antenna.

Generally speaking, a copper coating can protect the antenna from interference from the screen, but how much copper leaf did we need? Where did it need to be positioned? In the simulation, we could try out many different shapes and positions, and we were able to come up with an effective solution: a copper barrier in the middle of the phone, with a specified outline, area and grounding connection. When we manufactured the part, and tested it in real life, our predictions were validated. All the signal that the screen had eaten before was suddenly restored to the antenna!

We were proud to see that every antenna we redesigned using our simulator now performed to design specifications. Our phone users were able to have the best of both worlds: an inspiring FullView Display screen and connection quality that they could absolutely rely on.

Sound channels, electromagnetic fields, heat dissipation … In every field where they have been applied, simulators have come up smelling of roses. Our sound simulator modelled the propagation of 360° sound, and helped us optimize music input signals and the design of every cavity in the phone's body, so that the resulting sound output is rich and resonant. Our electromagnetic simulation of static electromagnetic fields enabled us to create solutions so that invisible and untraceable static fields would not interrupt calls or the plugging in and removal of earphones.

The need for speed

Simulations were proving their worth in more and more areas, but in terms of speed, we were still not hitting the pace that R&D wanted. They would often call us, impatient for their simulation results. So we kept on trying to find new ways to automate the process by getting the computer to do the modelling and analytics.

But this was easier said than done. Computers could easily recognize simple 2D images, but a phone is a 3D object with a complex internal structure. If you don't tell the machine how to figure out the shape, where the eyes and nose are, so to speak, it would be stuck making wild guesses.

We were stumped for a while by this problem. But I thought, there's no point simply grinding away at a problem we don't know how to solve. We should look at what is available in the industry. Any tool with the right kind of functions has got to be worth a try. I was chatting with a PhD who told me about a computer vision program they had developed at his research institute to recognize construction vehicles and block them from entry into restricted areas. When I heard that, my eyes lit up. "If it can recognize trucks, recognizing a speaker, or a microphone inside a phone should be simple, right?"

We quickly set up a joint research project with the automation research institute, and got to grips with the complexities of 3D computer vision. We were able to take their technology and adapt it to our needs, but for a computer to remain intelligent it has to keep on learning. The conventional approach is for people to prepare the training data to feed the machine. We took an innovative approach of combining simulation with machine learning, so that the computer could learn from anything the simulator could simulate. It made the training process smarter and faster.

Our simulator data analysis was also slow and difficult. For example, a single simulation involved 'dropping' the virtual phone from 26 different angles. It produced 26 sets of results, each containing dozens of gigabytes of data. It was extremely time-consuming to look through them one by one to find the maximum stress points. We defined rules for analytics and enhanced our algorithms so that one CPU handled the analytics for each calculation. With dozens of CPUs running in parallel, we could speed up the process dozens of times over.

Then, a single round of simulation took only 12 hours to complete, and in 2018 that time would be further shortened to eight hours. That means that the engineers can suggest a new design idea, and a full set of simulation tests can be completed the same day. This enables fast iteration of designs so that we can achieve the very best results – something that engineers in other companies can only dream of.

Unlike product features, the benefits of high-quality simulation are not immediately visible to end users. Nonetheless, simulation is a powerful development tool. It enables Huawei R&D to move faster than anyone else in the field and develop products stronger than anyone else. Soon, we intend to have our simulations become even stronger, so that any design we come up with can be immediately optimized, and we can deliver a better experience to our customers.

16

Dedicated to Making a Better Phone

By Bian Honglin

For the last few years, I have been responsible for hardware R&D. In my position, quality control is a vital issue that must be addressed systematically. It must be made part of phone development from initial ideation through to full production. To make sure this happens, we set up a five-layer network of quality checkpoints: design checks, testing, material checks, production checks and user feedback.

But we have known from the start that catching problems and stopping faulty phones from getting into the hands of customers is only the most basic goal of a quality system. What we want was something better: giving our consumers higher-quality smartphones. Because of this, we have progressively tightened and raised our quality standards, so that we are now working at a level far higher than the general industry standard. In fact, our standards are now higher than the industry's very highest. I am very lucky to be working for a large company like Huawei, because when we ask for technology and financing to improve quality, we have always received what we need.

Of course, Rome wasn't built in a day, and quality is not a problem with a single answer. All we can do is inch forward, day by day, toward the goal of making better phones.

Depth of technical expertise

In 2013, we received a piece of bad news. Some of our customers had reported that after using Huawei phones for less than a year, their phones would suddenly die after being plugged into the charger. The screens went black, and the phones would not switch on again. These were tailor-made phones for local markets. We promised our customers that we would fix the phones, and rushed them back to China. When we took them apart in the lab, we found that the charging chip had burned out. The chips were made by a well-known global chip supplier, so we sent them back to the supplier, hoping that they could give us some explanation for how this happened.

However, the supplier gave us the same reply twice: "We cannot completely explain this fault." The answer only came when I was chatting to a friend who worked for a different phone maker.

He told me that his company had found that every phone that used this kind of chip had the same problem, more or less. No one in the industry had the technical chops to determine the exact cause of the fault, so the issue was just something that everyone had to live with.

But Huawei is made of sterner stuff. We have served our operator customers for 30 years, and become elbow-deep in making and testing the telecom industry's most complex and finely calibrated products. This unparalleled experience could now be applied to our mobile phones. We also had a very large R&D team, with a proven capacity to develop fundamental technologies. Even my own background was actually in network equipment R&D.

So, we had exactly the skills needed to find the hardware flaw that resisted diagnosis. I set up a team to take on the job, and brought in some colleagues from our high-tech 2012 Labs. After getting permission from the chip supplier, I gave the team a suggestion to get started: if we peel open the chips, layer by layer, then examine every layer, we should be able to see what the problem is. Of course, actually doing that is not as easy as it sounds. Doing a post-mortem on a chip that has totally burned out requires the skills of a specialist. At the time, there were not many labs that had the ability to do this work in China. Most phone makers never do it.

The process took us more than six months. Each examination took a week, and we had dozens of dead chips to cut open. Finally, I got a phone call and heard an excited voice cry out, "We've found it!" I ran over to the lab, where one of our R&D crew pointed to a hole on an electron microscope image, so small that the naked eye could never see it. "Look, this is the substrate layer. The current burned a hole straight through it, and caused a short circuit. It's electrical overstress. The problem is the chip's EOS(Electronic Overstress) robustness." Now that we'd found the problem, fixing it wasn't too hard for Huawei's R&D team. The solution could be built into the next generation of phones, and from that day forward, Huawei never had a problem with its charging chips.

From this story, you can probably tell that the way Huawei does things is very different from the way most companies in the industry work. When we find a problem with a component, like any other company Huawei asks the supplier to work out the issue and resolve it. But if the supplier can't solve it, Huawei doesn't stop there. We use our own technical resources to solve the problem, then give the supplier the new standards we need them to apply.

I'll give you another example. Another of our phones died unexpectedly. It turned out there was a bit of bad soldering between a wire and the circuit board. Every supplier we asked told us the same thing: "That's just how it is with current technology. There's nothing we can do!" But for Huawei, that is not an answer we can accept. Customers are not interested in where the problem arose. Any problem with a phone is Huawei's problem. So, we invited three experts from Finland to come and look at the production line and calibrate every process and manufacturing parameter. In the end, they fixed the problem. This problem involved only a single type of solder flux, one of more than 100 used in the phone. Most companies only test the components, because if they are broken, they can be sent back to the supplier. But Huawei is determined to understand all of the different types of solder and their properties.

Why go to all that effort? Because we believe that when you make a phone, you have to do more than just buy the components from suppliers and slot them together. You have to understand every part of the product you make. You have to know it inside and out, and control all of the details that may seem insignificant, but in fact can have a serious impact on quality. That is the only way to ensure that you can make a good product.

Of course, we have the capacity to do this. If we didn't have the technical skills, then we would not be able to achieve what we set out to do. In fact, we are always building up our basic engineering capabilities, investing heavily in human resources and the tools we use "under the hood." This investment helps make Huawei stronger overall, and it makes it possible for the quality of every phase in our phone manufacturing process to get incrementally better every day.

After all these years,
my biggest takeaway is
that quality is more than
just a sense of duty or a
personal commitment to
quality slogans.

Investment brings results

There was a period of time when I couldn't sleep well. Often, it was because news of some problem on the production line had come through. I would find myself starting awake in the middle of the night. We shipped millions of phones every month, so any problem, even if it only held up the line for a day or two, could affect hundreds of thousands of products. So, in 2014, we started to build our Eagle Eye system: a system that would control every step of our phone manufacturing process. This meant all problems could be caught and handled internally, and we could avoid ever selling a faulty phone to our customers.

At first, we focused on controlling two main sets of data. One was the production data, which told us exactly what was going on at every stage of every production line, in real time. As soon as our first pass yield or our FMECA (failure mode, effects and criticality analysis) showed any variation, the system sent an alert so that we could intervene directly, and prevent any large-scale abnormalities from developing. The second set of data was from after-sales repairs. Whenever we start to see more faults of the same type than average, an alert sounds, and we scramble into action. First, we go and analyse the problem, to see which batch of phones is the issue, or whether there is a problem on one of the production lines. Then we urgently work on a solution.

I thought at first that with a two-level data control system there would be enough to get us very close to zero accidents … But one incident made me determined to add a third layer of defence to the Eagle Eye system. It was during 2014 that a colleague called me and said in a very urgent voice that the Eagle Eye system was reporting a huge number of quality issues in a batch of one particular phone. "How many phones in this batch?" "300,000!" Now I could see why it was so urgent.

The fault was in an inductor component made by a supplier, a tiny thing no larger than a sesame seed that is very common in mobile phones. We used over ten million units of this component every single day. In the phones where we had identified the problem, short circuits in the induction circuit made the phones unable to perform properly at certain frequencies. Not all users would use these frequencies, but we couldn't simply sell the phones as-is and hope! Instead we identified the 300,000 phones affected and quarantined them. Even worse, this inductor was underneath the shielding cover, which had to be removed during repair. The success rate on the repair was low, so the entire circuit board had to be replaced. But these boards cost about 1,000 yuan each. In the worst-case scenario, all 300,000 boards would have to be replaced, that would mean losses of ¥300 million! I nearly broke down crying when I realized the size of the problem.

We started testing the affected batch one by one. Thank goodness, only a small percentage actually had the fault, and the vast majority had no problem. At this I started to relax a little, but the episode was a warning for me. Eagle Eye had done its job, and discovered a problem early enough that we could intervene and stop any faulty phones from reaching our customers. But it would have been much better to discover the problem earlier. During peak times, our production lines work at a rate of 500,000 to 600,000 phones per day. Even the slightest problem can cause extremely expensive delays.

Following this incident, we decided to roll Eagle Eye out with our suppliers as well as in our own factory. This meant the suppliers' production data for the electronic components they made would be directly available to Huawei. The slightest variation in quality, and we could send in a team to ensure that not a single faulty component slipped through. Everyone would benefit. Customers could be confident in the phones they bought; Huawei could have confidence in the components that flowed into our manufacturing process; and the suppliers did not have to worry about having to compensate Huawei for faulty components.

Now we had three levels of control: one over production of components at our suppliers; one over our own production facilities; and one over after-sale repairs and maintenance. It was a truly all-seeing network of quality control. In quality control, you can never quite eliminate all problems. That would be unrealistic, since the world always throws curve balls. But our Eagle Eye system gives us the power to catch faulty phones, and to offer our customers something better.

The author, Bian Honglin, checking phone quality data

Of course, nothing in life is free, and the cost of the Eagle Eye system was considerable. As far as I know, the system we have built is the only one of its kind in the world. Virtually no other companies were willing to spend this much money on their quality systems. Huawei has always been willing to invest in quality. For example, in the early days of phone manufacturing, certain tests were carried out by hand and, as we know, human process are always going to be error-prone. This is an unavoidable truth of quality control. In the end, Huawei invested about 800 million yuan in the development of a system that could automate most of our quality checks. It would complete tests like accelerated ageing and audio testing. The equipment worked extremely well and made a big improvement in our phone quality.

Sometimes I hear colleagues talking among themselves, wondering if all this investment in quality systems is really worth it. After all, it drives up product costs. I believe that it is definitely worth the investment, because quality is one of our fundamental principles. Quality is our brand and our reputation. If we fail in quality, then the customers will give up on us.

Leaving industry standards far behind

Unlike with telecom equipment, some functions in the mobile phone industry do not have globally accepted standards – for example, drop tests or minimum working temperature. After researching how consumers actually use their phones, we found that some of the standards that are commonly applied couldn't guarantee that the phones will stand up to normal usage. So, where necessary, Huawei sets its own higher standards. We often joke about it: our phones clearly meet the standard that all our competitors are using, but we had to go and raise the bar higher – we're just making a whip for our own backs!

For example, the standard phone test for high temperature requires the phone functions normally at 60°C and 90% humidity. We changed that standard to require it continuously functions at 85°C, 85% humidity for 240 hours. These numbers were not just plucked out of the air. They are derived from an actual case of product failure that we investigated.

In 2015, as I monitored Eagle Eye, I noticed that the after-sales repair data was showing an uptick in phones within China that would no longer turn on. We analysed those phones every which way, but for a long time we couldn't find the cause of the fault.

One day I suddenly noticed that the problems seemed to be occurring more often in the summer than in the winter. I had a flash of inspiration: if there is a pattern over time, might there be a geographical pattern as well? I called in the girl who does the data analytics, and asked her to sort the faults by geographical area and display the results on Eagle Eye. When the image popped up, I gave a whoop. The little red dots were clearly clustered in a few areas like Chongqing, Hunan and Hubei. This geographical clustering was bound to give us a clue.

But what was it? Did users in these areas use their phones in some different way? No. So the only possible factor had to be the local climate. We carried out more tests, looking at acid rain, dust and any other issue we could think of. Gradually we locked in on one key issue: all of these places had hot, sweltering summers. When some of our phones were being used in hot, humid conditions, the circuits just burned out after a while.

All of these phones had passed the 60°C/90% humidity test, so clearly that test was not giving us enough information about the products failure potential. You may be wondering how that could be. After all, 60°C and 90% humidity is a very extreme environment. Why would that test miss this problem? The reason is the length of the test. Although 60°C/90% humidity is an extreme environment, the test phone was only in the environment for a few days. The faults didn't have time to develop. When we put in place our new 85°C/85% humidity test standard, a number of other potential problems were exposed. We found that for every 10°C increase in temperature, the number of faults doubled.

With the 85°C/85% humidity test standard, we started to see corrosion and cracking. Our dedicated R&D team helped us find the causes, and then we talked to the suppliers about improving the components. Many of them were shocked by the standard we were asking them to achieve. "You're crazy!" they said. When they said "crazy," they meant two things. First, they didn't understand why Huawei would want to force them to meet a standard far higher than the industry standard. Second, high quality like that was certain to increase our costs. The suppliers didn't have the technical expertise to solve many of the newly discovered problems, so at this point we had to deploy some of Huawei's considerable R&D resources and engineering expertise. We researched solutions ourselves, made the necessary breakthroughs and then passed them on to the suppliers.

Another example of Huawei's higher standard is button durability. The industry-defined standard is that a button must stand up to one million uses, but we did not apply it. We set the test rig to keep on pressing the button many more than one million times, until the button failed. Then we analysed the reason for failure, and corrected it.

Why is Huawei so committed to high quality standards in every aspect of our phones? The answer is simple: so that our customers get a better phone to use. I personally think of it like this: every year we ship more than 100 million phones. If we only applied general quality standards, then a fault rate of just one in 10,000 would still leave us with more than 10,000 customers who would have a bad experience. That is not acceptable to us, and so we are taking deliberate action and raising our quality standards.

That has now become the Huawei standard procedure: applying quality standards beyond the normal levels to expose as many problems as possible, using our deep well of R&D resources to analyse and solve the problems along the way, passing our solutions on to suppliers, and driving the entire industry forward.

After all these years, my biggest takeaway is that quality is more than just a sense of duty or a personal commitment to quality slogans. It is a complex and systematic endeavour, involving many different specializations. Every step in the production process requires attention and expertise to be built up over time. Every improvement requires the investment of substantial funds, if you want to lift standards above the industry norm. My colleagues and I spend our lives putting together better phones for our customers. That is our professional pride as part of the Huawei Consumer team.

Mobile Phones and Me:

A Story that Was Meant to Be

By Fang Fei

Many people first became aware of Huawei phones when the Mate 7 was launched in 2014, but our phone-making history actually extends more than a decade before then. When we started out, the phone industry was monopolized by firms outside China. Huawei's first ever phone was actually made to support the sale of our mobile network base stations.

Village connector shows Huawei has phone chops

In 2002, many of China's less-populated regions still had no mobile network coverage. Huawei had launched a piece of network equipment called the CDMA 450, which would help extend network to underserved rural communities, but we soon realized that we also needed to provide a phone that would work with this network equipment in order to provide a full service.

At the time, I was working on the Wireless Network Product Line, responsible for testing 3G systems. When the company decided that we needed to build a phone, I was assigned to the team, along with Wang Yinfeng and a few others, and we set up Huawei's first phone R&D team in Beijing. We were called the "fixed wireless terminal development team." There were just ten of us at the start – enough to fill a single big table in a restaurant. Our mission was to create Huawei's first ever piece of user equipment, which would be called the *cun-cun tong* or the "village connector."

The first generation of the village connector was a wireless fixed terminal with an antenna that could be connected to landline telephones. It was designed to serve villages with no connection to the phone network. I was in charge of the software at first. This whole area of mobile phones was new to me, but I read a few papers and then dived straight into the development. It was a real case of learning on the job.

In fact, all members of the team were learning as they went along. After three or four months, we had put together a prototype. I remember there was an issue about radio frequency paths that took us half a month of serious work to resolve in the lab. The first time we managed to make a successful call through our new system happened to be the last day of 2002.

We broke for the Chinese New Year, then just as we came back to start work, we were interrupted by the outbreak of SARS. In April 2003, a few colleagues and I were visiting the lab in Shenzhen. We planned to head back to Beijing at the end of the month, but everyone who arrived in Beijing from southern China was being held in quarantine. We decided it was better to stay in Shenzhen and continue our work there.

The epidemic in Beijing was serious and, in many parts of the city, schools and offices were closed. But our work never stopped. Everyone was determined to get us over the finish line, and to launch Huawei's first foray into the user equipment market.

In mid-2003, we finally completed the product, and took it to Tibet for the first trial. Many of the villages in Tibet's ranching county had no telephones at all. We rode a big truck from village to village, delivering our phones to the herders who lived there. They were shocked at our arrival, and some rushed out with thick red cloths to wrap up the precious new arrival, lest they get bumped, scraped or muddied. We quickly explained that this was not a good idea, because the machine needed to keep cool. It would be fine standing there unwrapped. It felt like a real achievement to put those expressions of happiness and wonderment on the faces of these village residents, as they carefully handled their new equipment.

Later, we also brought out a new generation of the village connector that actually looked like a telephone, and added multi-RAT technology (Multiple Radio Access Technology) to it. That product ended up being a big seller, shipping to places as far off as Algeria and India. This was a good start that clearly showed Huawei had the ability to develop phones. We had made a good start in the user equipment market, and I had officially become a part of Huawei's Consumer BG.

Opening the door to cooperation

Huawei's Consumer BG continued to progress in phone development. We consistently invested in R&D for feature phones and other products. During this period, a major event changed the face of the industry: in 2008, Google released the Android operating system for mobile phones.

It was game-changing for everyone, and it offered a glimmer of hope to Huawei. We had been battling through the feature phone market for a few years now, and the biggest problem we had was with our basic software. Now that there was a brand new, open source operating system that could challenge Apple's iOS, we had the opportunity to compete on even terms with all the other big smartphone makers. If there was ever a time to go all out, this was it.

My team had experience developing feature phones and wireless fixed terminals, so the leadership gave me the task of leading the development of a Huawei Android smartphone.

I had mixed emotions about this new project. That year, I was 33 years old. I had been hoping to slow down a bit at work and have a baby. Now I had been assigned another mammoth task by management. For Huawei's Consumer BG, smartphones would be a completely new venture. We didn't know how to develop them, didn't have a predefined market and the team assigned to me was very small. I had no idea how to lead this team onward and upward.

So, should I turn down the assignment? I hesitated for a while, but when seeing the level of trust that my managers were putting in me, I put aside any thought of refusing and, with that, the job was mine.

Developing a product is no theoretical business. The first question I had to answer was: did Huawei have the ability to join the Android alliance? Today, this question sounds laughable, but back then it was a real hurdle that we had to jump.

We had not yet had presence in the mobile phone market, and when I visited Google's Android manager, the first thing he said to me was, "What kind of a company is Huawei? Do you even make phones?" Even though I explained till my lips cracked, he didn't seem to have the slightest interest in working with us. How could we demonstrate our capabilities to Google? I called the team together and we racked our brains. Finally, we came up with an idea: at that time, phones had two chips, an application processor and a modem. If we could program the Android system into a phone with only a modem, that would prove we had engineering capabilities not seen elsewhere in the industry. When I took the phone that we had produced to the Google Android manager, he was very surprised. Not only that, he conceded that Huawei must have a serious engineering advantage after all, and from that point on Huawei and Google have worked together.

Once we got our Android licence, we began to build up our roster of talent. But it wasn't easy getting the human resources we wanted. Everyone still thought of Google as a website. Many people working in the industry in China didn't think that Android had much of a future, and wanted to wait and see, rather than cast their lot in with a developer of Android phones. But we kept at it and, after much searching, we pulled together a team to build smartphones.

Huawei's first smartphone

Building the team was only the first step in a long process. If we wanted to retain our team, we would need to make some money – and where was that going to come from? Who was going to buy our phones?

After many years in the telecom market, I had the feeling that there were opportunities in Europe. Europe's telecom operators were aggressive and ambitious. They were open to new ideas and new technologies. So, we asked the marketing team to take us to meet up with T-Mobile, the mobile arm of the German telecom operator Deutsche Telekom. We told them all about Huawei's vision for smartphones. I made a slide deck to show them our understanding of Android, our product concepts and our strong R&D team. We planned to produce a smartphone, similar to an iPhone, with a large, 3.5-inch screen. We would also team up with the company that first developed the soft keyboard, and brought in a top-flight design company to work with us on the interface. Our innovative ideas and unique approach finally captured T-Mobile's interest.

In February 2009, at the MWC in Barcelona, T-Mobile announced that it was working with Huawei. I was both anxious and excited going into that event. I was excited to have a customer at last, but anxious because this product now had a seven-month delivery deadline. At that point we were only at the concept stage, and the team had only 50 people. There was simply no way to get from concept to product in that time.

But now the agreement was signed, and we had to deliver. Not just that, we had to deliver something truly competitive if we wanted T-Mobile to stick with us.

Our problems were not limited to our lack of people. We were also experiencing interference from inside the company. The Procurement Department didn't want us to use capacitive touchscreens, because Huawei had never worked with suppliers in that industry before, and because they had to deal with a lot of patents. The combination of patent risks, tight delivery schedules and new supplier risks was just too great.

But I insisted on using capacitive touchscreens. My reasons were very simple: smartphones were the future. Resistive touchscreens (which require the use of a stylus) were a technology of the past. If we settled for second best on this issue, then our product would be dead on arrival, with no chance for success.

So, we were committed to using capacitive touchscreens and, if there was risk, then we would just have to deal with it. I took the head of Huawei's Consumer BG with me to meet with the Procurement Department about what we could do to minimize patent risks and prevent any other supply risks. We found two suppliers and tested their products. In fact, we worked with them to solve a number of technical problems with their touchscreens. Then we asked Procurement to set up a liaison team that could work with them to resolve any other future risk.

To keep our development costs down and make the product more competitive, we unofficially 'borrowed' a number of people in other departments to help us with engineering the phone. They also took part in the debate early on over how we could develop an improved design based on our existing hardware.

But the biggest challenge for our team was T-Mobile's orders for customized technology on their phone. T-Mobile wanted to give its users a better experience, so it requested a number of technologies that were still relatively unproven. We had to get together a team of key R&D employees, product managers and systems experts to engage in several rounds of meetings with T-Mobile, to analyse what they wanted and conduct market surveys, so that we could test as we developed, and gradually build up a better picture of what we needed to achieve.

Huawei was actually one of the very first Android phone makers. There were a number of teething problems in our partnership with Google. T-Mobile worked with us on these problems. They would talk to Google for us to ask for help and support, and generally assist with the development of the phone. Our team was very short of staff, and our skills were quite limited. Every night I got home at 1 or 2 am, and for several months it all felt like stumbling around in the dark. The light at the end of the tunnel was not yet visible.

I ran myself ragged those days, telling everyone in other departments that smartphones were the future for Huawei, and that we were laying the foundations for Huawei's smartphone range, and we would be very grateful if they could contribute just a little bit more … I had everyone who had any personal connections to use them, and to scrounge together every resource they could. I even brought over ten people from the Indian software team to Beijing. It was all-hands-on-deck to get this project done.

Finally, all of the support and effort paid off. We made Huawei's first ever smartphone, the Pulse, on schedule, and received warm praise from T-Mobile, well known as one of the most demanding customers in the industry. They said, "We are very happy with Huawei's timely delivery, which demonstrates that our selection of Huawei as our partner to produce the T-Mobile own-brand phone was correct."

From that point on, we continued to expand into the European market. Within two months, we had received orders for 100,000 units, and the phone subsequently went on sale in the United States, where it sold nearly three million units. Gradually, the smartphone market was opening up to Huawei.

Affordable smartphones

Our first smartphone had sold in the low millions, and had attracted positive reviews from all our customers. But we still had some way to go before we were firmly established as a smartphone maker. At that time, most of our phones were produced for operator customers. What operators wanted was good value: low prices plus good performance. But we ran into a significant problem. Chip makers were not giving us the support we needed.

The chip makers wanted to force us to buy more expensive, newer chips, so they refused to offer upgrades and support for new Android releases on older chip series. This meant that we could not easily bring the cost of our units down. Backed into a corner, we made a tough decision. If the chip makers wouldn't support us, then we would make the necessary software ourselves.

I grabbed some of our best guys from the software team, and started looking into how it might be done. We quickly realized it wasn't as complicated as we feared. It was just an issue of making sure the chip's underlying system was compatible with Android. We quickly identified the key changes and solved the problem.

In order to better understand our customers and give them a better experience, we did a survey of university students to find out more about their preferences. Based on what we learned, we made a sporty little phone called the C8500, with a 2.8-inch capacitive touchscreen, bright colours and a sports car-inspired dynamic design. This won us an order from China Telecom. Originally, China Telecom was only going to buy a small proportion of their phones from Huawei. But as our phone proved more attractive to their customers, we ended up selling a lot more units than we expected on this order.

And we continued to pursue the very best in phone design. We were determined to make a phone with a 3.5-inch screen that offered similarly great value for money. In order to cut down on the thickness of the phone, we went so far as to compare the thickness of various paints and coatings. We pushed specifications, visual design, colours, performance and the user experience to the limit, and were ultimately able to produce a phone that could meet the needs of large telecom operators around the world, whatever kind of network they were on (CDMA, UMTS and so on). The 3.5-inch screen was surrounded by the world's narrowest frame at that time, and the price was kept to within 1,000 yuan.

This phone, the C8650, was named the Sonic and came out in 2011. Sales were brisk around the world – in fact, we'd never had such a big seller. The whole team was sent to help suppliers resolve production and testing issues.

Our suppliers devoted an entire floor of production space to turning out this one Huawei phone. In one of our tests, we have to play the phone's ring out loud, so during the peak of production on that phone, we had ringtones ringing out throughout the building from morning till late.

I remember one production problem took a lot of time to figure out, so much so that we bought up all of the SIM cards in the nearby China Telecom stores, and spent the entire night randomly testing the latest batch. The phone regulator even contacted us because they couldn't work out why such a concentrated burst of calls was coming from our building in the middle of the night. Everyone arrived at the supplier's early every morning to fix whatever issues had arisen in production, and when we got back to the office, we met to discuss and find solutions.

In the end, the Sonic became Huawei's first phone to top ten million in sales. We had shown the industry what Huawei could do, and that we were willing to invest money and human resources into R&D for smartphones. From that time on, Huawei was on the right track to become a mobile phone powerhouse, which would pay off with the development of high-end smartphones, including the P series and the Mate series.

Proposals, Mansions, Broken Hearts and Hard Deadlines

By Yang Yinan

In the depths of a 2016 night, a shrill ringtone sounded, waking me up out of my sleep in Huawei's staff residence in the United Arab Emirates (UAE). I blearily answered the phone.

"They've all disappeared! They're all gone!" The voice on the other end was going a mile a minute, and clearly in a state of great agitation. Still half asleep, I peeled open my eyelids long enough to focus on my watch, which said 2.45 am. Who could be calling at this hour?

"This is Ali. I've got a problem. You have to come and help!" Ali was one of my oldest customers. He had bought every Huawei phone from the P1 to the P7, and had called me before to ask for help with phone problems. But I had never heard him panic like this. I composed myself and tried to make sense of his broken description. Trying to calm him down, I told him to come to my office in the morning, and with that, he finally seemed to relax a little.

The next morning, I arrived at the office and saw Ali waving me over in the distance. The receptionist told me that he had been waiting there since 7.30 am.

My colleagues and I told him to stop worrying, sit down and have a drink of water. And gradually we got the full story of what had happened from him.

It turned out that Ali had lost his phone somewhere in the city over the weekend. He had tried everything he could to find it, but it was like looking for a needle in a haystack. The phone was lost for good. Of course, a phone could be replaced, but the photographs on the phone were quite a different matter. Those photos contained some of Ali's most precious memories of happy times with his girlfriend.

He was just about to propose to her, in fact. They had been dating for many years, and Ali had it all planned out: he would have his photos edited together into a video of their romance as the high point of the proposal. This romantic gesture was sure to melt her heart, but now his raw materials were lost and he was going crazy!

We started asking some detailed questions, and found that Ali had previously used a Huawei account and the HUAWEI CLOUD app. I was relieved to hear that, and told Ali with a smile that although we may never find his phone, we could recover his photographs. Ali looked at me suspiciously, saying, "Really? That would be amazing."

I sat Ali in front of the computer, and opened up HUAWEI CLOUD. Unfortunately, he couldn't log in. He had forgotten his password. He tried possibility after possibility, but none of them were correct. Beads of sweat started to stand out on his head, and he looked increasingly anxious. I could see that things weren't going well, so I got him a glass of water, and tried to calm him down. We thought about other possible approaches.

Could we try the password recall function? I prayed under my breath that he had his login name right, at least. As it turned out, he did. Ali's cloud account was linked to his email, so he was able to send a password reset link to himself, and finally he logged in to HUAWEI CLOUD. This service backs up our users' private information on the cloud, including their photographs and their contact lists.

When he saw the photographs he thought had been lost, he unfurrowed his brow at last. He repeated over and over to me, "Shukran! Shukran!" ("Thank you" in Arabic).

Once we had recovered his photographs, we talked Ali through the cloud backup function in more detail, so that he knew how to put his important information on the cloud in future. So long as he could remember his login, he would always have access to his data, wherever he was in the world.

Not long afterwards, Ali called me on the phone, his voice full of undisguised happiness. "She said yes! We're getting married!"

I have been working at Huawei for nearly ten years now, always in posts related to consumer service. I have met many customers like Ali, who have ultimately become my friends. Ali's phone call sent me on a trip down memory lane ...

It's not easy having a big house

Back in 2012, after four years working at HQ, I was dispatched to the Middle East. My first assignment was in Oman. This was not my first visit to the region. I had worked there for two short spells previously. It seemed that fate had decided that my future lay here.

Huawei was only just expanding its consumer business into Oman at the time. Sales were limited, and the market was largely untapped. There were only two Chinese employees on the consumer team. We had to set up a service team and take care of all the other work, including testing and delivery of goods. As our sales increased, we also methodically built up our team. Customers vary from country to country, but Huawei's customer-centric principles remain the same. I have always believed that when we provide services, we are servicing not the lifeless device but the living person. We must always put ourselves in the customer's shoes, and treat them with integrity, if we are to win their trust.

I was once invited as a guest into the home of a local customer. His house was near the sea. It was a large, three-storey villa. As I admired the view, I noticed that he was using a Huawei wireless router. During our chat, he mentioned that the router did not have the range that he had hoped for, and that he got no wifi signal in his bedroom on the third floor. If he wanted to watch TV or a movie while lying in bed, he had to use mobile data.

Wifi does indeed have a limited range. A single router is usually enough for an average home, but for a large house with three storeys, I would not expect a single router to be enough.

Huawei had recently launched a new wifi repeater specifically to boost signal in this kind of situation. It could boost wifi coverage, and act as a wifi relay. I quickly described the product to him, and recommended that he try it. My detailed description of the product and its specifications made him very excited, and he told me he wanted to buy one straightaway. He took me to a nearby shopping mall, and picked up five wifi repeaters. I was rather shocked, and tried to give him a friendly reminder that for a single property, two repeaters would definitely be enough.

"My son lives right next door," he replied, "and he has the same problem! I'll get some for him as well."

We set the wifi repeaters up in the two houses, and quickly configured them. We then found that every room in the house now had an excellent wifi signal. Even lying in bed, the customer would now be able to connect to the wifi network. The customer and his son were both very pleased, and told me many times that I must return and visit them often.

Repairing a broken heart

All good things come to an end, and two years later I said goodbye to that house by the sea, and moved on to a new phase in my Huawei Consumer journey.

In 2014, I was transferred from Oman to the oasis in the desert that is the UAE, where I would work in Dubai. The UAE was quite different from Oman. It was a much larger market, with many consumers. I focused on services and delivery. We set up a user services centre in Dubai, where we completed all of our repairs. Every week, I had to visit the service centre and all of the other Huawei stores, which gave me an excellent opportunity to talk to our consumers and get their responses to our questions.

On 14 February 2018, Valentine's Day, all of the malls were decked out in romantic decorations, and sales were everywhere, proclaiming it a day of love. But for us, it was just another day at work, and we still had to visit the stores. In the early afternoon, I walked into a phone store in Deira, and spotted a Chinese couple arguing with a shop assistant over something.

I saw that they were both very agitated, red in the face, and the shop assistant was clearly at his wits' end trying to control the situation as he explained something over and over to them. I quickly walked over and asked what the matter was. It turned out that Ms Xu was a businesswoman who travelled frequently between China and the UAE. In her hand, she held a P7 phone which would not turn on, and she had come to the store to have it repaired. The P7 had been launched in 2014, and was now no longer in production. The store didn't carry the parts for this model any more, which meant that they could not repair it. Ms Xu would be returning to China for a meeting that very afternoon. She needed to leave for the airport in a little over an hour.

Huawei's Consumer Services Centre, UAE

We explained the issue to her patiently, but Ms Xu was very disappointed. She had used her P7 for a long time, and even though she knew it was an old phone, she couldn't bear to get rid of it, because it had half of a heart engraved on the back, with the other half on her boyfriend's phone. The engraving was a special service that Huawei offered when you bought a phone at a Huawei flagship store. You could have the design of your choice engraved for free on the back of your phone – either a design suggested by the store or a design you drew yourself. It was like giving your phone its own customized tattoo.

I turned the phone over, and there on the back was half of a heart. The man standing next to her was her boyfriend, and on his phone was engraved the other half.

Clearly there was a clash here between the earnest desires of these customers and the lack of hardware in the store. How could this difficult situation be resolved? Based on my principle that we serve the people, not the phones, I immediately called the nearest repair store. The phone repair specialist hurried over, and a quick inspection revealed that the problem was with the battery. He made a call to get a new battery sent over immediately. By this point it was not long before Ms Xu's plane was due to take off. She was worried that if she waited any longer, she would miss her flight. If she didn't wait, then she would be travelling without a phone, and she would have to send her phone in for repairs again. And that battery was already on its way …

Years of customer service had taught me to always put myself in the customer's position, and to aim for a full solution. The repair would not take more than half an hour. If Ms Xu was worried about her flight, she could go and check in at the airport, and I could bring the phone to her once it was ready. There would be plenty of time. When Ms Xu understood my plan, she nearly jumped for joy. She gave me her boyfriend's phone number, and the two of them rushed to the airport. The phone was repaired shortly after 3 pm and the owner of the store drove me to the airport in his own car at top speed. Finally, I was able to deliver the phone to Ms Xu before her plane took off. She was immensely grateful, and kept thanking me over and over.

On this Valentine's Day, I was proud to have been able to give the gift of love to this couple in Dubai.

Seven days means seven days

Of course, not every encounter with customers goes so smoothly. Sometimes customers are angry, but I never let their anger affect my mood, because it is precisely these points of friction with the customers that show us how to improve the quality of our products and services.

"I only bought this device two days ago! And this problem has happened at least twice already!" In early 2018, the P10 was launched. I had only just stepped inside the door of Deira's largest electronics store, when I saw a Huawei sales promoter staring at a P10 in puzzlement, with an angry customer complaining to her. I hurried over and asked what the problem was. There was a problem with the P10's App Twin function, which lets a user maintain two WhatsApp accounts and two Facebook accounts on the phone at the same time. It was developed specifically for the needs of businesspeople in the market outside China, who might have separate accounts for work use and private use.

The customer's name was Mohammed, and his primary accounts were fine, but on his secondary accounts he could not watch any videos sent to him. The promoter and I tried several times, and the problem was clear. I couldn't solve the problem there in the store, so I spoke with Mohammed and assured him that we would do our best to resolve the problem within a week.

The customer had barely left the store when we asked all sales promoters in the local VOC (Voice of the Customer) management group to check for this problem. The R&D, maintenance and testing teams for the P10 were mainly based in China, so it would probably take a while to gather all the people we needed to solve a problem like this. I sent an email to everyone involved, asking them to meet the next day for an emergency session.

At 7 am, as I was still on my way to work, my phone was already dialled into the conference. The problem involved software and the third-party app compatibility teams, so HQ estimated that it would take at least ten days before a new update could be released. But I had already promised my customer that we would get it done in a week. We couldn't disappoint the customer. To solve this problem, we increased the grade of the trouble ticket so that the version manager could launch the emergency processes, and demanded that the R&D team produce a demo version for testing within a week.

I followed up with reminders every day, and on day five, just before we got off work for the day, I finally received the demo version. It was the middle of the night in China when the R&D team sent it out. That night, at 9 pm, I was able to call Mohammed, and tell him to meet me at the Service Centre the next day. But he wasn't even willing to wait one night. He demanded that we fix the phone there and then!

Half an hour later, at the Service Centre, he and I both watched his two WhatsApp accounts successfully receive and play back videos. Mohammed's face split into a big smile. "Good!" he said. "Good!"

The story continues ...

In what seems like the blink of an eye, I've spent over five years in the Middle East. I have many stories like the ones above. There have been calm and reasonable customers. There have been more than a few driven half-crazy with frustration. For many, their problems were solved quickly. For some it took a little more time to produce a solution. There is no such thing as 100% perfect service, but we have to approach service with a 100% positive attitude. I know very well that customer complaints can seem overwhelming, but no matter what the customer says to us, we must always take it seriously, and take responsibility for helping the customer. The service journey is long, and we still have a long way to go.

Ali, my friend in the big house, Ms Xu and Mohammed are just some of the happy memories that I have stored up. And the story of me and our customers continues.

Rising Star

By Anson Zhang

The nomadic peoples of ancient Europe used to burn a mark into the backs of their horses so that they could tell whose was whose. These ancient imprints (*brandr* in old Norwegian) gradually evolved into the brands of today. Now, our goal in building a brand is to create an imprint on the hearts of consumers.

Since I started working in Malaysia at the start of 2016, I have been wondering: if Starbucks represents elegant surroundings and a lifestyle of leisure, and if Nike is the epitome of speed, fashion and youth, then what mark does Huawei imprint on the hearts of consumers? And how can we make that imprint deeper and faster?

When I arrived, Huawei was just another little-known foreign brand in Malaysia. It felt like you could count the number of Huawei phone users on the fingers of two hands. That was the situation when I started working in the consumer market in Malaysia. The first problem we faced was how to boost customer recognition and brand awareness among local consumers. The hardest part of any project is getting started, so I said, let's knuckle down and get this brand out in front of people.

One day, I was having lunch with my colleagues, when we bumped into two Malaysians, and started to chat. They were both using phones from another brand, and I asked them in confusion: Huawei makes great phones, so why would you choose this brand? Their answers shocked me. They mentioned over and again the slogan that this company plastered across its advertisements. I had seen this slogan, and thought it was a bit obvious. But it had clearly made a deep impression on people, and had won their brand-new fans. Huawei's advertisements tended to use rather lofty language. It lacked that directness and realism. This brief discussion made me think again: do we need to change the language that we used in our communications?

Rather than puzzle it out for ourselves, we could simply learn from the best examples around us. I decided to study how other international brands advertised themselves. I found that many brands changed their language when they came to Malaysia. For example, there was a Japanese manufacturer of air conditioners which used very majestic language in its international ads, but in Malaysia the slogan just said, "Made in Japan, best in Japan, Japanese quality." It had used this slogan for years, and sold very well.

There were many similar examples. Why was it that the Malaysian market required this kind of a change? I talked to local customers and our Malaysian staff, and discovered that Malaysia is a trilingual country, with Chinese, English and Malay all in common use. All of the languages were used in a simple way. For example, the English used among locals was much simpler and more direct than how people speak and write in Europe or America. So many brands changed their language to become more plainspoken for Malaysia.

Once I had understood this, I started to introduce more localization into the advertising of the P9 smartphone after it was launched. I used simpler language so that consumers could understand us at a glance.

A good brand starts with a clear narrative

Say it clearly, do it effectively, don't get bogged down in grand visions or constantly changing slogans, and stimulate consumer need … This was what we needed to do.

The HUAWEI P9 was launched in Malaysia in June 2016. The P9's breakthrough feature was its photography. It had a Leica-certified dual camera, which put it ahead of any other phone in the market. And I had read with surprise a survey that found Malaysia is one of the biggest regions for uploading photos to Facebook. The locals here love to take and share photographs.

Clearly, the P9 was a perfect match for this market. I was determined to use the most direct, clear advertising language to explain these technological breakthroughs. So "Leica Dual Camera" appeared all over the city.

We got the message across, and it was a very effective piece of messaging. The P9 became a very popular phone in Malaysia, a hit right from the start. We communicated its core value by emphasizing the dual cameras, and the campaign imprinted the idea firmly in the minds of consumers. Now, whenever Huawei was mentioned, I found that consumers knew: Huawei has the powerful dual cameras.

Once I was in a taxi, and chatted to the driver, he told me that his son had a Huawei phone.

"Why does your son have a Huawei?" I asked him.

"Because Huawei phones are great for taking photos!" He gave me a big thumbs up.

Sales of the P9 were ten times higher than sales of the Mate 8.

Less is more in branding

The P9 was selling well. Now, our mission was to use our new fame to boost our whole range of products. Our marketing budgets were going down, and our rivals were spending several times more than us. How were we to ensure that we made an even bigger splash with the Mate 9 and P10 when they came?

We knew that the value of any new functions or specifications would be gradually eroded over the course of the product lifecycle. But accumulated brand value could be used to support several generations of phones. And the consistent delivery of brand messaging can help the messaging of future products have more impact. We therefore kept the "dual camera" in the advertising for the Mate 9, P10 and Mate 10. We made photography the key brand feature that drove sales of the entire series. For the Mate 9, we used *High Performance Dual Camera*; for the P10 we called it *Dual Camera Evolution*; and for the Mate 10, *Dual Camera with AI*. Ultimately, we were able to turn this messaging into brand value, as our customers gradually began to associate the Huawei name with continuous innovation.

As well as the camera innovation, we also worked on establishing Huawei as a global brand, by showing off Huawei's position in the Fortune Global 500. Many places build landmark buildings or statues, so that people will remember a person or a historical event. Brands are just the same. One ad that stays in the mind of users can have ten times the impact of other ads. So we started to fight for better placements of our ads. The placement we had in mind was the best spot on the major way to Kuala Lumpur Airport. We started negotiations through our advertising procurement agency, but it was unable to obtain the spot for us. I was tempted to give up at that point, but in the end I called up the owner of the billboard slot himself, and we were finally able to make a deal. So, in the month when the P9 was launched, our "Leica Dual Camera" advertising finally appeared, in Kuala Lumpur's most prestigious advertising slot.

This helped lend more prestige to the Huawei brand.

Outdoor billboards on the way to Kuala Lumpur Airport

"We've seen your ads. They finally look like the ads of a major company." The impact was immediate. Distributors who had lacked confidence in Huawei before now sought us out. Even other phone suppliers started commenting on how sneaky we were in obtaining prominent advertising slots, and hoped to learn how we did it.

International brands must localize

During one promotional event, I surveyed young consumers, and found that a number of people replied that they didn't know anyone who used a Huawei phone, so the brand felt distant to them. It was not a brand that got close and spoke to them. As a result, they didn't trust it. The simple, direct advertising language had helped them get to know Huawei. But how could we make the brand seem more familiar?

For a product, familiarity is an emotional tie to the consumers.

Malaysia is diverse ethnically, culturally and linguistically. So we needed a marketing plan that tackled that cultural and linguistic diversity head on.

In September 2017, we launched a major new product, the Nova 2i. The campaign surrounding this product was designed for Malaysia's diverse needs. Young Malaysians love local stars and local music, so hiring a Malaysian brand ambassador would have

The high-intensity strategy worked. Recognition of the nova brand shot up over the course of just one month, and the nova took a much bigger market share than any Huawei phone before.

a much bigger impact than using an international star. We decided to choose a rising young name, hoping that we could grow in fame together.

One of the most popular new stars in Malaysia is Hannah Delisha. She is an actress on a hit TV show, loved by her fans and has plenty of potential to grow even more famous. She already had a large local following, and we judged that she was just about to have her breakout moment. We therefore asked her to become the first Malaysian star to sign up as a brand ambassador for Huawei. Together, we signed a long-term growth agreement that tied together her personal image with our brand image, and agreed that we would combine our resources for brand communications.

We also invited a well-known local musician to write a catchy Malaysian pop hit to celebrate the release of the nova, and asked Hannah Delisha to star in the music video. That would play on all the local TV stations, to increase awareness of the new phone.

In Malaysia, TV stations still retain large audiences. In the past, we had placed ads in every different place we could think of, but had never achieved the results that we wanted. The reason is that you need a level of advertising intensity in order to produce an effect. In the past, we had spread our resources too thin, and so never really penetrated our viewers' consciousness.

This time, we put 80% of our advertising resources into our key channels like TV and cinema ads.

The high-intensity strategy worked. Recognition of the nova brand shot up over the course of just one month, and the nova took a much bigger market share than any Huawei phone before.

Helping customers know us better

Our market surveys found that though consumers are constantly bombarded with ads, many people still know very little about tech products, and have no way to distinguish high quality from low quality. Huawei phones offered not just the dual cameras, but also a long battery life, good operating system and excellent manufacturing. How could we help consumers get to grips with this information?

We made improvements in display cabinets. Our phone display cases had always had a simple white-on-red Huawei logo. This did nothing to catch the attention of consumers. Now we have turned this logo space into a mini poster, and developed a series of "Did you know?" talking points. They include, "Why a dual lens takes better photos," and "Why Huawei's quick charge function is safer." We use a few short lines to explain key Huawei technologies. This helps us create new selling points for future phones.

But for consumers, the information is hard to trust, because it comes from us. We needed a third-party organization that could give an objective comment. Many media companies could provide persuasive assessments of products, and a lot of consumers watch or read product reviews in the media. But the Malaysian media are often unwilling to be critical.

There are several local websites that produce technology reviews, and when they heard about our plan, they were very interested. We provided new phones to the reviewers, along with our customer handbook. We asked them to compare and review our phones, but we would not look at or interfere with the results. They produced a test report that assessed the phones from multiple different areas, and used easy-to-understand language to explain how comparable phones stacked up against each other. As a result, our technological advantage really stood out, and consumers started to recognize our strengths. The websites got bigger audiences as well, and other media have since followed suit with more technology reviews.

By early 2017, phone reviews had become a key marketing feature of the Malaysian phone market. By working with the media and other third parties, we have given consumers a more comprehensive understanding of our phones, and helped them make the right purchasing decisions. Surveys reveal that tech reviews are now an important factor when consumers buy a new phone.

A rising new star

In two short years, we transformed the Huawei brand from a distant stranger to number six on Malaysia's list of most popular brands, and the number one fastest riser on that list (source: You-Gov Brand Index 2017). We have leaped to become the rising star among Malaysian brands, and we have seen a big jump in our sales revenue as well.

The answers to the questions that I asked when I had just started working in Malaysia are now becoming increasingly clear. But we also know very well that the consumer market is a constantly-shifting domain where competition is fierce. We must remain tightly customer centric. The road ahead is steep, but I believe it is full of hope.

For Elise

By Hu Jian

It has been seven years since Huawei's tablet first hit the market. Back in 2010, our team consisted of just seven members, based in Wuhan. In 2017, we are aiming to become a top-three player in the global tablet market. Our flagship tablet – the M series – is now in its third generation, developing from the M1 to the M3. It has finally clawed itself out of the red and into the black, and is now making a profit for the company. This is the result of our constant and consistent efforts to make the best tablet in the Android ecosystem.

The HUAWEI MediaPad M3 won over a dozen awards, including the Best of IFA, at the IFA Berlin 2016 trade show

Climbing out of the red

"Hey, I hear you work on tablets at Huawei. I want to buy a tablet with a high-resolution screen and excellent specifications. What do you recommend?"

A couple of years ago, this would have been a hard question for me to answer. I was not confident in our own products, and I worried that my friends wouldn't like my recommendations. The word "tablet" was barely even used back then: everyone just said "iPad," because it was number one in the market. How could we carve out a space for ourselves in this sector?

In 2014, after a long period of experimentation, our M series tablet was born. We wanted to deliver the ultimate entertainment experience in both video and audio. But nothing comes easy, and we encountered many difficulties along the way. With the M1, our big idea was about music brightening your life; with the M2, it was all about a sleek appearance and inspired experience. But somehow we were always behind our competitors. When the M1 was launched, we were drowning in criticism: "The specifications are too low"; "I hate the large black border around the screen"; "It's just a big phone."

It was very worrying for our team, and led to low morale among our key developers. To make things even worse, the development of the M2 was far behind schedule. Due to low sales, the M series continued to bleed money. The atmosphere was very sombre.

As the project manager, I was unsure which way to turn: did we have to return to the old model and just make low-end products? We were feeling our way through thick fog, unable to work out which way we should be heading. As we struggled to find our way forward, the smartphone team went from strength to strength. The Mate and P series phones were huge successes because the company picked the right strategy. We were constantly asking ourselves, "How can we make an Android tablet that measures up to the competition?"

We regained our confidence under the leadership of our product manager Min Gang. We tried to extract the lessons learned from the first two generations of our tablet, and developed better unique selling points for the third generation: an inspired entertainment experience with audio and video. We named this third iteration of the M series Beethoven.

Is it better to use the best components or the right components?

It's not easy to make an Android tablet that stands out. In the fast-changing world of smart devices, the boundaries between tablets and phones are blurring. The main difference is simply the size of the screen. That's why we wanted to give our customers an immediate, impactful and inspired sensory experiences with our M3 tablet.

First things first, we needed a good screen. But what exactly makes a good screen? Does it mean it has to be better than other screens in every way? At the end of 2015, the project team had divided into two camps, with different views about which parts we needed to procure.

"Our M3 must outperform our M2 by at least 30% in all key display indicators, such as colour saturation and brightness," insisted Chen, our multimedia engineer. "Otherwise, there is no way we can compete in the market."

"The screen must be no thicker than 2 mm," said Wang, the industrial design engineer. "We want the display to be slim, but with the highest specifications possible. Let's use Material A – it's the best material there is."

But Procurement rejected all of these proposals. "Material A may be thin and of good quality, but the price and supply terms are not within acceptable margins. Consumers won't pay the high prices these materials will demand. This is not an option for us."

The two camps argued and argued. It seemed that we couldn't find any overlap between acceptable costs and high-performance components. As the project manager, I was torn between the two viewpoints, until Min Gang, our product manager, pointed out something during yet another deadlocked meeting. He said, "Good products do not have to be expensive, nor do they have to be number one in every technical metric. Are there any other solutions?"

This question made us think back to our original vision. What we wanted was to make an Android tablet that customers would recognize as the best on the market. We didn't need to make a super-expensive luxury item. This realization drove my colleagues and me to find the optimal solution. Finally, we came up with a solution that would perform well in key indicators and deliver a unique user experience.

To make the device as attractive as possible, we aimed for the best possible screen. We kept a 2K-resolution display for an instant, excellent visual impact and detailed, textured images. We also introduced a colour enhancement technology invented by our 2012 Labs, which produced hues as close to natural human vision as possible.

But this would not be enough to convince consumers to choose us. Our research found that repeated, intense exposure to screens could cause eye fatigue. Therefore, if our tablets could embed a blue-light filter, it would be a new selling point. We offered clarity of vision and protection of the eyes to address an important pain point for our users. It was achieved through unique but inexpensive features like smart dimming and a blue-light filter.

But would customers buy it? As it turned out, our advertising slogan, "clear vision and eye protection," caught the attention of device shoppers as soon as the tablet hit the market. According to our user survey, the M3's high-resolution screen and rich screen colour were among users' three favourite features.

Looking back at our journey, we never gave up. I became more convinced that to develop great products, we needed more debates, more discussions and more relentless focus on what our customers actually want.

The Beethoven development and delivery team won a Huawei Team Gold Medal Award in 2016 (author, Hu Jian, second from the left in the front row)

Scrambling to fix a tiny crack

Without sound, a show loses one of its biggest assets, and a movie will struggle to capture the audience without voices and music. This was the idea that inspired the name "Beethoven" for our third generation M3. We wanted our users to have an experience equal to a Beethoven symphony when they listened to audio on their M3.

We partnered with Harman Kardon, the industry's top audio brand, on our M2 tablet back in 2015. The results of this were clear – both user feedback and market outcomes were positive. We were certain that we wanted to keep this feature in our M3. But how? It wasn't easy to pack such great sound into such a small tablet.

One quiet Friday evening, the calm in my apartment was broken by an urgent phone call. It was Zhang, an engineer working on the production line. He said, "We're getting interference in the audio quality tests here on the production line. There is feedback when we test the microphones, and the defect rate is at 5%! We have halted production, and we need to sort this out as soon as possible."

Upon hearing this, I was wide awake, and had a sinking feeling in the pit of my stomach. Feedback was a complex problem, involving different audio components, product design, internal insulation and assembly processes on the production line. We needed to resolve the issue immediately; otherwise, this would affect our stock and timetable for the product launch.

Given the tight schedule, Lin, who was responsible for the M3's audio module, rushed from Shenzhen to our Huizhou factory overnight. Lin analysed lots of data and tried to identify the root cause: "This indicator is approaching its limit ... Another indicator has exceeded 1 dB."

We analysed the data of one unit after another, and then tried to identify some patterns. At the very outset, we thought there was a problem with the microphone. So we replaced the microphone components, but the defect rate was unchanged.

So, we wondered if it could be a problem with the seal around the microphone jack. We used glue to tightly seal any cracks between the body of a faulty tablet and the microphone, and tested it again. The results were still no better.

We were stuck. Then Lin came up with an idea: "In my experience, feedback comes when you have internal structural issues.

Get a microscope and compare the shapes around the microphones in the good and defective tablets." Using a powerful magnifying glass, we finally identified the cause to the problem – the rubber sleeve around the microphone did not fit snugly. That was it. This tiny hole was to blame for everything.

So we added an extra washer underneath the rubber sleeves to tighten it, and the problem was finally solved. Our products passed the quality tests one unit after another, and the production team started smiling again. The blackboard was full of crazed scribblings, and as I looked out the window, I realized it was morning.

All the hours spent tracking down and eliminating just 1 dB of feedback were finally paying off. With Super Wide Sound, developed by our 2012 Labs, the M3 was able to deliver stereo sound equal to that of two stacks of speakers. The hi-fi sound was nicely balanced between bass, mid range and treble. In the end, we passed the strict certification tests set out by Harman Kardon.

Adding a front fingerprint scanner

We wanted to place the fingerprint scanner on the front of the tablet, as this was what users expected for large tablets. But we did not have any experience with this architecture, so we had some concerns.

Our product architect, Zhu, raised several questions: "Our competitors all have scanner buttons, which are simply screwed onto the casing, while we use touch scanners, which are faster. However, our tablet doesn't have any casing at the front, so we will have to glue it onto the screen. Is that possible?"

Feng, who was responsible for structural design, was worried, too. "It's difficult to keep defects low when you use adhesives. Our suppliers have never done this before, so I'm not sure what results we'll get with this design."

I gave the team the boost that they needed to move ahead. "Our competitors have managed to develop tablets with front scanners, and we can do the same!" I knew that the design would involve many challenges, but they were not insurmountable.

We had no experience, so we had to figure it out as we went along. We tested all parameters for the whole process, confirmed their effects and built up our own first-hand data. Building on this, we were able to determine the factors that would determine success or failure in each process. Then, we analysed and compared how to attach the scanner, and checked key factors like the adhesiveness, contact surface width, surface mount technology (SMT) and contact surface smoothness.

Each test required collaboration between many different teams, including production procedures, architecture, production technology, structure, scanner components and hardware. We visited our supplier many times to check our experimental data.

We introduced a long-term reliability test to monitor whether all fingerprint scanners were securely attached to the screen. At the very beginning, nearly all the scanners failed the test, dropping off after extended use. We continually improved on this, and the failure rate gradually dropped from 50%, to 30% and then to 0%. The scanner was slowly pushed in to become increasingly flush with the surface, so that it protruded by just 0.18 mm, then 0.16 mm and then 0.15 mm. We tested a dozen types of glue, generating hundreds of thousands pieces of data. Our supplier joked, "We've turned into a branch of Huawei R&D!"

We finally achieved our goal of having a reliable front scanner, and were able to give our customers a familiar device with a smoother finish for a better experience. We also analysed customer complaints about Huawei devices' virtual navigation. Following a suggestion by Richard Yu, we combined the scanner with the virtual navigation bar. This meant we no longer had a virtual navigation bar taking up space on the screen, giving our customers a better screen experience.

Taking pride in user feedback

No pain, no gain. Our hard work finally paid off. At IFA 2016, the M3 won the Best of IFA award along with ten other awards. We got 98% positive feedback online, putting us first among all tablets. The tablet has sold well since its launch. In the past, I was afraid to recommend our tablet to my friends. Now, it's the only tablet I can recommend, and our users also help spread our brand. It has been a great journey.

I hadn't thought much about the name Beethoven until one customer mentioned it to me. He was very interested in the name, and asked, "*Für Elise [For Elise]?*" I was stunned, and thought "Aren't our customers our Elise?"

We have worked hard to explore how to develop the best products and deliver an inspired experience to our customers. We put customers at the heart of everything we do and make the most trusted tablets for our consumers. To this extent, we have achieved what we set out to achieve.

These ten years working on tablets have flown by. Our team has grown, gathering new members from around the world. We started as a seed of an idea in the Wuhan Research Centre, and that seed has sprouted and grown tall. We have remained committed to our vision, and have made it a reality. Our tablets still have much room for improvement, and we are still some way behind the industry leaders. But anything is possible as long as we believe. In 2018, we started afresh, with the aim of becoming number two or even number one in the world tablet market.

Creating a Cosy and Inviting Space for Customers

By Yang Jian

What do customers see when they walk into a Huawei retail store? What do they hear? What do they like and dislike? These are some of the questions that we, the retail management team for consumer devices, keep asking ourselves.

"I come in when the store is well lit"

Light is not something that you can touch, but it directly affects the customer experience. Does the store look like a premium brand? Do the items on the shelves look attractive? How long do customers want to stay in the store?

What type of lighting is most comfortable for the eyes? Is the best lighting actually lighting that customers never notice? A few years ago, we didn't give these questions any serious thought. We just bought standard LED strips as required by the company. Later, the company introduced standards for in-store lighting, but they were generally just copies of the national standards for commercial lighting.

In August 2016, we started trying to figure out how lighting works and why. We combed through books and websites on interior design; we studied lighting standards developed by authoritative bodies. We were amazed by the great deal of research on the subject: there are more than 50 different parameters that you can use for lighting. Take colour temperature and illuminance, two of the most common parameters, for example. Colour temperature varies according to the light source: incandescent lamps produce warm light whereas fluorescent lamps give off cool light. Illuminance is another critical parameter. The higher the illuminance, the brighter everything looks; but when illuminance is too high, it can be uncomfortable to look at. By fine-tuning these parameters from different lights, we can transform the look and feel of a space.

Good lighting is vital for a retail store

We also picked up innovative lighting ideas from shopping malls, bars and restaurants. For example, Starbucks uses a great number of spotlights in their stores. The spotlights are meticulously positioned, spaced from each other with great precision. These spotlights are adjustable 360°, and they are arranged so that there is never direct light shining on your face, no matter where you sit or what direction you are facing. This way, customers do not feel uncomfortable.

Our research taught us many clever methods for avoiding annoying lighting. For example, frosted glass can be installed to reduce glare, or low-glare lights like downlights and spotlights can be used. To measure the right amount of lighting that customers feel most comfortable with, we acquired two illuminated signs from a supplier and had them installed in our test store for consumer devices in Beijing. One was left unchanged at the original manufacturer settings and the other was modified so that we could adjust the illuminance to the environment. We adjusted the lights until we had the setup where we felt most comfortable, and then we recorded the parameters required to produce that state.

After that, we were able to give suppliers exact parameters instead of subjective and vague instructions for them to follow. We now inspect our suppliers' factories every month, bringing light meters and other devices with us to make sure that all light boxes are made to the right specifications, so that we can consistently provide our customers with the most comfortable in-store lighting.

"I don't want a phone with nothing to play"

When customers walk into a Huawei store, most of them go straight to the counter to play with the demo phones. But in the early days there was not much to play. There were only a few apps such as the microblogging app Weibo, and you could not connect to the internet. There were no games, either. So all customers could do was to take a few pictures.

We were determined to change that. What do customers want to do on demo phones? The first thing they like to see is the specifications of the phone. Some brands put detailed specifications in an app and allow customers to compare different models. That gave us inspiration. For the P10 smartphone, we developed an app that guides customers through the various features of the phone, such as the wide aperture mode and front fingerprint scanner, to provide them with all the technical information they need.

But customers want much more than hard data and statistics. They also want compelling stories that stir their emotions, stories that they can relate to. Why not create stories for our customers, recreating events that might happen in their lives when they use the contacts, messages, memos, calendar and other features?

We gathered the creative types and set up a team to develop the script. Say your wife's birthday is 9 December; you open up your contacts, send a message to all your family and friends to invite them over for the birthday party on Sunday. You put your shopping list, hotel reservation information and the birthday party menu in the memo app, set a birthday reminder in the calendar app and record the precious moments of that day using your phone.

We implemented the new app on the P10. It was the first time we had tried to explain the value of Huawei phones to our customers using specific, real-life scenarios. They might not remember everything as they went through the app, but the storyline let them feel the features that were created for them to enjoy.

What other apps would be fun and useful when customers were test driving new phones in the store? We sent out questionnaires and used the simple and laborious method of downloading the top five apps in every category from the app store. We tried all of them out and selected the best ones. When it came to the parenting apps, our team of child-free bachelors downloaded and tested each one, picking up a lot of useful knowledge for the future! In the end, we loaded 11 apps on the demo Mate 10, including Zhihu (China's Quora), Bilibili (China's YouTube) and Anipop (China's Candy Crush). Previously, customers might swipe the screen a few times, then wander away, unimpressed. Now, with the apps to play with, our customers are spending more time with the demo phones!

A huge crowd in the store

We are going to move further and follow the latest trend in the industry. We plan to connect our hundreds of thousands of demo phones to the internet. It might not be long before customers are able to play King of Glory, multiplayer online battle arena, with their buddies in our store. Going forward, we will deploy artificial intelligence to enable customers to talk to our demo phones, further improving customer experience.

"Can we make the phone display stands invisible?"

Phone display stands are everywhere in a store. In addition to holding up phones for people to look at, display stands also charge the phones and include anti-theft security devices. However, these useful stands also cause frequent annoyances. When customers put the phones back on the stand after they finish looking at a phone, the phone often falls or slips, sometimes causing the alarm to go off. This can be startling and cause a poor experience for the customer.

So, we wondered: do customers really need the display stands? Are they happy with these restrictive and intrusive devices when they are trying out a phone? If not, we should make them disappear or become invisible.

We started working on the quality of the stands and reducing the annoying false alarms. A display stand has three main components: the anti-theft device, adapter (power supply) and coiled connector cable. When our supplier inspected the faulty display stands that we sent back, they found that most of the false alarms were due to faulty coiled cables. The cable usually consisted of 120 tiny wires. When more than 30% of these wires were damaged, there would be false alarms. We worked with the supplier to address the issue: more wires within the cable, thicker insulation, and connector hoods where most of the wear and tear occurred, making the cables more durable. We also changed the screeching siren to a gentler sound.

We then worked with the supplier on ideas for making display stands invisible: "We need to make them invisible to customers, so it's best to use transparent material." "Yes, they have to know a display stand is high-quality just by looking at it." We tried many different materials before settling on acrylic plastic. The non-acrylic part was white – the same colour as the counter – so that it blended in seamlessly with the overall colour scheme of the store.

However, over the past two years, consumers have become increasingly interested in phones with glass backs but which easily slip off the stands. To address this problem, we changed the angle of the stands from tilting back to standing up. What's the precise angle that made customers feel most at ease? Our questionnaires provided important data: customers generally stand 10–20 cm away from the counter, and considering the average height of a Chinese customer, we decided that 75° was the best angle. Having the phones standing up offered two advantages: it was easier for customers to pick up and put down the phones, and it allowed customers to see the back of the phone.

The new display stand

How could we make the stand even better? Many customers wanted to see the price and technical specifications of the phone at a glance. Could we display the information on the stand? We drew our inspiration from the Freshippo supermarket in Beijing, where they have a massive range of products and use electronic price tags. This means the prices can be changed using a computer. We quickly got in touch with a vendor of electronic price tags to implement the idea.

We have now finished the prototyping phase and will pilot the new display stands later this year [2018]. Next, we are shifting our focus to wireless anti-theft devices and stands embedded in the counter. We believe it won't be long before the stands completely disappear, giving customers a carefree feeling as they try out the phones.

"I like gifts that are unique"

In additional to the phone itself, customers often ask store assistants if they can get a gift if they buy a phone. The cups and key rings we used to offer were often met with frowns: "That's a bit cheap! Not attractive at all."

What were customers' favourite gifts? That was the question that we were asking in the summer of 2017 before the launch of the nova 2. We visited many stores to research their promotional gifts – we took a close look, felt the quality with our hands and asked a flurry of questions. We made so many visits that eventually store assistants from the entire neighbourhood knew who we were.

After our research trips, we held multiple brainstorming sessions: nova 2 was due for release in June. What would young people be doing at the height of summer? Most would probably go on vacation or be playing sports. What would they need on vacation? What gifts would be useful when they were playing sports? By asking question after question, we were able to get inside the customer's mind. We soon decided on a trendy sports water bottle and an umbrella that would be both cool and useful for active young people.

Young people today like unique products, and men and women might prefer different gifts. We decided to create two gift packs. We put a sports bottle, a tangle-proof data cable and a decorative ring grip in the gift box for men. For women, we bundled a mini travel umbrella, a selfie stick and a mirrored ring grip. We put the gifts into different coloured boxes: azure for men and pink for women.

What else did customers want? They wanted a gift box that was easy to transport and access, so we used one that featured a drawer. We asked more than 100 store assistants to rate the packaging and selected the best box style.

When all details were confirmed, it was less than a month before the new product hit the market. Under the time pressure, we monitored the production line closely and managed to have the gifts delivered to all the stores before 16 June 2017, when the nova 2 was launched. The phone was a big hit, and we waited anxiously for feedback from our salespeople. Our WeChat group exploded with pictures of the nova 2 and – to our amazement – of the gifts that we prepared. Customers loved our gift packs! Our supplier told us that after our huge success, many other brands were now coming to them and asking questions.

Later, we repeated a similar process for the Maimang 6 and the Mate 10, using gift packaging that was closely related to the products and aimed to deliver the best customer experience. These gifts may look insignificant, but it was worth doing our best on them.

We always have to put ourselves in the shoes of our customers and figure out the details from their perspective. That's how we know what they're thinking. We hope that every customer that walks into our store will sense our warmth, dedication and care so that the Huawei brand can take root in their heart.

The MateBook:
Living Up to Its Name

By Zhu Chencai

On 20 February 2016, while China was celebrating the Spring Festival thousands of miles away, my teammates and I were in Barcelona, preparing for the annual Mobile World Congress (MWC).

The sun was shining brightly in a clear blue sky outside our small hotel. But we were not in the mood for sightseeing, only sitting silently on the ground. On the bed lay our brand-new MateBook laptops, ready to be unveiled to the world. We had not slept for days, but no one seemed to feel tired. We were extremely nervous and could only ease the tension by polishing and testing our demo products over and over again.

The night before the launch, when we were having dinner together, Mr Yang, president of the product line, pointed to the Columbus Monument and proclaimed, "Over 500 years ago, after Columbus discovered the New World, this city was where the news was first received. Today, this city will also be the first to witness whether our product line can discover and open up a new world."

On 21 February, we launched the MateBook, a brand-new Huawei product. The product immediately sparked intense discussion: it looked like a tablet, but was larger and featured a leather keyboard cover. This light and handy device was powered by an Intel Core processor and ran the standard Windows 10 OS, a combination that had never been seen before.

Discussing the launch event and presentation in a hotel room in Barcelona

Every one of the 1,200 available seats was filled at the launch event. After the presentation, people swarmed around our five experience stands to try the new device. We had to bring out dozens of extra demo devices to make sure that everyone got a turn. The first HUAWEI MateBook laptop was one of the highlights of the MWC.

Since that day, Huawei has officially been a manufacturer of laptops, and the MateBook has become increasingly popular.

Why MateBook?

The first thing some people think of upon hearing the name Mate-Book may be the HUAWEI Mate series of smartphones. Since the laptop's core customer group partially overlapped with our smartphone customers, using a similar name made it easier for consumers to recognize the new product. But that was not the major reason behind the name. Two years earlier, when the product initially took shape, we came up with many possible names, like SlimBook, FashionBook and HuaweiBook. In the end, we chose MateBook, because we wanted our laptop to be our customers' best mate, just like our high-end smartphones. We wanted our laptops to be more than just tools that would be taken out when needed and shelved at other times.

The first HUAWEI MateBook won several awards at MWC 2016

What is a good product? After many rounds of discussion and clarification, we identified the elements that should make up the MateBook's DNA.

First, it must be beautiful, which meant offering users a high-quality visual, audio and tactile experience. It should be both enjoyable to use and a symbol of elegance and sophistication.

Second, it needed to be easy to use. Users should find it convenient and useful, and it should offer a consistent and interconnected experience in all usage scenarios. It should also help consumers benefit from the latest technological advances by integrating new technologies into the product as soon as possible.

Once we had nailed down this combination of features, it sounded great. However, making this a reality was easier said than done.

Fine details leading to beauty: 0.6 mm thinner after a drink

At the end of May 2015, we finally completed the initial design of the MateBook 2-in-1 laptop. After numerous rounds of prototyping, simulation and testing over nearly six months, we finally reached a consensus regarding the goals of the overall design and specifications. However, just when everyone started to think we could take a break and begin preparing for the next phase – product development – I discovered that the current design would leave the product 0.6 mm thicker than our goal. What could we do? Was it better to compromise, or insist on the original goal?

The team members spent the whole afternoon deep in discussion. Most people took a conservative perspective. They pointed out that 7.5 mm was already 1.6 mm thinner than our main competitors' products, and was also thin enough compared to ARM-based tablets. So there was no need to make it a further 0.6 mm thinner at the risk of putting more pressure on the heat dissipation system, which was already close to its limit. Only the industrial designer Zhai was unwilling to compromise, and for just one reason: an additional thickness of 0.6 mm would disrupt the harmony of design. After so much effort, we had achieved our ideal form factor in terms of length, width and rounded corners and sides. If we then compromised on thickness, the overall appearance would be completely changed. It would disrupt the harmony of design and thus was unacceptable. However, when we asked exactly how the design would be disrupted and where the difference was, he could not give us any precise data. The atmosphere became tense and the meeting ended without agreement.

That night, we went out for a drink together. We initially thought this would help us relax and think outside the box. But following the intense discussion in the afternoon, everyone was just eating, without talking or drinking, and the atmosphere stayed tense. After a while, I went around the table raising my glass and drinking with each person individually. This finally defused the tension. We soon drank two full crates of beer in less than 15 minutes, and everyone started to loosen up. The sounds of clinking glasses, laughter and happy shouts filled the air. We looked back on the hardships of developing our first product together and looked forward to the future of the new industry. We became quite emotional and some even shed tears. Finally, we reached a consensus: our first product must take the world by storm, so the core industrial design specifications must be reached without compromise!

Our heat engineer Zhi promised right away that he would leave no stone unturned in his effort to meet the heat dissipation requirements – and if he failed, he would quit! After that, he immersed himself in solving the problem and earned himself the nickname "thermo bro."

Looking back two years later, our no-compromise approach was worthwhile. The appearance of our first product shocked the industry. The upgraded version further optimized the heat dissipation system and ensured that our product's leading edge in appearance could last for at least three years. We set new benchmarks in the industry.

Going the extra mile to ensure ease of use

Classic two-in-one products have fingerprint scanners, but apply completely different design concepts. On Apple's iPad Pro, the scanner is on the home button in the middle below the screen. On Microsoft's Surface Pro, the fingerprint scanner is on the right of the keyboard's touchpad. As a newcomer, if we used one of these two mature solutions, the risk and investment would both be smaller. However, our industrial designer Zhai and chief PC archi-tect Gao were unwilling to stick to the established practices.

They believed that a two-in-one product was different from a traditional laptop, as the keyboard was detachable. If the finger-print scanner was installed on the keyboard, it would be useless when the device was being used without the keyboard. In addi-tion, two-in-one products with the Windows OS were usually held horizontally. With a 12-inch screen, the fingerprint scanner would not be reachable when the user was holding the device with both hands, no matter whether the key was on the long or short side. This would negatively affect user experience. In addition, considering our product's very high screen-to-body ratio, making a hole for the scanner would make the product look less appealing. So neither of these two designs could give users the best experience.

Therefore, we abandoned the two designs that were commonly used in the industry. Instead, we decided to borrow the design of a Huawei smartphone and put the fingerprint scanner on the side, between the volume keys. This would ensure consistency across our product range, and make the scanner easy to locate. However, as the product frame was extremely thin, the available area for the fingerprint scanner was very limited, so the scanner's accuracy was very low at first. We had to order our own customized fingerprint modules, which was unprecedented in the industry. After many debates and reports, and much back-and-forth with suppliers and experts, we finally delivered the function. But I still had a question. With the Windows OS, using fingerprints to unlock the device would take three steps: pressing the power button, then pressing Ctrl + Alt + Delete on the keyboard, and finally unlocking the device using the fingerprint scanner. What was the point of such a function? Especially for our two-in-one product, the keyboard was often separated from the display. This meant the user would have to use the keyboard in order to use fingerprint recognition, which was less convenient than just typing in the password. This design would not work. We needed to offer the same experience as mobile phones to unlock the device with just one touch within seconds.

The moment I said this, the experts were taken aback. "How can a computer be exactly the same as a mobile phone?" they asked. "You clearly know nothing about the business!"

This was indeed a problem we had never had before: the sleep mechanism used for mobile phones and tablets was completely different from that used for Windows laptops. At that time, there was no technology for instant wake-up, so all PCs used the three-step solution. We turned to PC giants Intel and Microsoft for help, and their experts also suggested that we stick with the three-step solution. But we were not willing to compromise. Otherwise, our design would completely deviate from the original goal of ease of use. Even though it had taken a huge investment of time and effort to make our fingerprint scanner functional, it seemed we would have to abandon it.

Innovating to achieve impossible dreams

We had invested so much money and effort into the fingerprint function, so the thought of abandoning it appealed to none of us. Even if the industry experts thought it was an impossible dream, we still wanted to make it happen. If there was no existing solution that we could copy, we would blaze our own trail. After all, many past Huawei products had achieved what people described as impossible dreams.

So we continued to experiment. After much research, we found that we could make a one-touch wake-up possible by adding a single microchip and using new Windows 10 software.

However, nothing ever turns out quite the way you plan it. A million things can go wrong when you are striding at the cutting edge of technology. Many of the features of Windows 10 were still extremely unstable, and often led to abnormal power consumption, overheating, wake-up failures, crashes and other problems. In addition, the implanted fingerprint wake-up function often failed to recognize fingerprints. As a result, unreliability was the main problem with our first MateBook. User complaints poured in, and some people within the company also began criticizing us. They felt we did not know enough about the industry. At that time, only Microsoft's Surface Pro and our MateBook used Windows 10. Some in the company also thought it was rash of us to incorporate the new function without a thorough technical analysis and sufficient preparation. They even questioned whether the one-touch fingerprint wake-up function had any value or, if it did, what that value was, and whether it was worth the risk of an unstable product.

The team was depressed by the problems, and we came under a lot of criticism. Some team members started to back down. They proposed that we give up on the function and return to the original solution – pressing the power button before scanning the fingerprint. But others insisted that since we had already created and promoted the fingerprint wake-up function in the first generation of our product, it would be too embarrassing to give up on it. But what could we do about the problem of instability? We had no idea.

To resolve this problem, our team worked hard for more than two months, and created several different prototypes so that we could compare the experience with each. After nearly three months of analyses and testing, we finally found another solution that used one microchip along with tested, mature technology. This solution would allow the user to unlock the laptop from light sleep mode with a single touch. The experience was as good as that of a mobile phone, and earned enthusiastic praise from consumers: "Perfect experience – exactly like using a mobile phone, easy to use."

This kind of recognition excited us and motivated us to continue with our good work. We then thought about whether the fingerprint scanner could be integrated with the power button.

The challenge was to address the logical relationship between the power button and the fingerprint scanner, and then the logical and sequential relationships between the scanner and button, as well as various Windows modes. We also needed to ensure a response time that would be acceptable to users.

Software architecture presented the biggest challenge if we wanted a simple user experience, given all the complex logical relationships. Our R&D experts and engineers developed 16 iterations, covering over 240 complex scenarios, to create the optimal solution: hiding the fingerprint scanner in the power button. With this solution, users only needed to press the power button as before, and the fingerprint scanner would scan their finger at the same time. This led to a very user-friendly experience.

It may feel like a small thing, but it represented a major technological advance ahead of our competitors. We had significantly improved the fingerprint scanning user experience on laptops.

This process helped us understand that in product design, more is less and less needs more. If users need to adapt, practise, think and operate more, they will be less pleased, relaxed and satisfied. To make it easier for our users, we must invest much more effort into thinking, developing and improving our products.

There is no best experience – only a better experience. Improvement is a never-ending process.

Two years later, the second generation of the MateBook X Pro made a splash when it appeared at MWC 2018. It once again attracted the attention of the global IT industry, and won nine awards from major international media outlets within two days. The innovative design of the 13.9-inch full-screen (first of its kind for a PC) and camera, hidden within the keyboard, offered a more attractive appearance and a more user-friendly experience.

Laptops used to be a symbol of high-tech and high-value personal consumer electronics. But 30 years after they first appeared, laptops are now lagging behind products such as mobile phones, televisions and cars in terms of innovation and experience. As a newcomer to this field, we hope to apply the technologies we have developed for smartphones, tablets and mobile broadband to laptops, bringing real value to users and inspiring the whole industry to innovate with us. For sure, our products still have some flaws. However, we will continue to improve, innovate and upgrade our products to improve user experience. This will ensure the MateBook can truly live up to its name and be a mate to Huawei customers everywhere.

23

The Lion's Share of a Small Market

By Su Jie

When we talk about Huawei's consumer products, I'm sure the first thing that everyone thinks of is the mobile phone. Not many people realize that Huawei is already the leader in markets across Europe, North America, Japan and other developed nations for another consumer product. It's a little product that doesn't attract as much attention: internet dongles.

We started selling these wireless attachments for computers in Europe in late 2005, and by 2008, our dongles were sold by almost all telecom operators on the continent. When I walked into a European operator's high street store in 2018, I was surprised to find that they were still selling Huawei internet dongles.

The sales assistant told me that many people in Europe still like using dongles to get online, because they are small and easy to carry, and can connect multiple devices. A certain number of people buy them every month.

The sight of this product that I know so well made me swell up with pride. Selling consumer products is usually like working in a fish market: you can only sell the very freshest produce. But internet dongles have been selling steadily for a decade now. It took me back to a time over a decade earlier, when Huawei Consumer was still struggling to keep the lights on. Back then, our biggest goal was simply to survive.

Top target: survive for two years

I remember that 2006 was a tough year for Huawei Consumer. Huawei had started making phones as a supporting product for our wireless network equipment. The mobile phone market was viciously competitive, and Huawei was a late entrant without any blockbuster technologies to give us an edge. We suffered losses for our first three years, and we had to borrow from other departments just to be able to hand out staff bonuses at the end of the year. The other consumer product lines were not making much money either, so morale was low across the board.

We needed to do something to turn the situation around, so we invited Company M, which was leader of the pack in the phone world at the time, to come and talk to us. We were unpleasantly surprised when the CEO of Company M responded by pouring cold water all over our ambitions. "I recommend that Huawei give up its ambitions in the area of consumer products, and focus on its network business. Just as consumers will only consider two brands of cola, they will only accept two mobile phone makers, and they are Company M and Company N. There are no opportunities here for other companies."

He wasn't grandstanding or threatening us. In fact, it sounded more like a friendly recommendation. Even some of our own managers were worried about the future of our consumer business. The company only had limited resources, after all, so perhaps it shouldn't waste them on R&D for consumer products that were going nowhere. Some suggested that the company should just sell off the consumer division.

But was giving up really the right thing to do? If we didn't, could we actually produce good consumer products? No one had an answer to these questions.

In 2006, 99% of the consumer market was still 2G products. Our competitors had strong brands and good technologies, so if we wanted to slice off a part of the 2G market, it would require massive investment of resources and a bloody battle for sales – and there was still no guarantee that we would emerge with anything to show for it. But the 3G market was wide open. Huawei was building out 3G networks for operators around the world, but there were not yet many 3G user devices on the market. Not many phones were able to connect to the internet, and mobile internet was still just a futuristic buzzword.

So, could we take advantage of this opportunity? Could we make 3G user devices and achieve success in this new market?

Once the suggestion was out there, the controversy began immediately. Some people said this was a crazy idea. After all, 99% of the market was 2G. If we gave up on 2G products, we'd be giving up virtually all of the market and betting everything on 3G. But when exactly was 3G going to happen? Others said that 3G networks were already being built on a large scale, so clearly 3G was going to be the next big thing. Rather than waste our time and energy bashing our head against the brick wall that was the 2G market, we should just focus on the 3G market, and develop competitive products that could give us an early edge there.

The only thing to do was
to overcome all difficulties,
and make it happen.

In the 2G market, we faced a tough battle. In the 3G market, we faced uncertainty, but we might just be able to find our niche and establish ourselves.

Huawei Consumer's management team talked it over and over, and finally came to a decision: we should focus our R&D efforts entirely on 3G devices. We were giving up 99% of the market at the time, and making a determined play for the market of the future. Huawei set up a specialist WCDMA (Wideband Code Division Multiple Access) team in Beijing, a CDMA team in Shanghai, and a dongle team in Shenzhen. The goal was to achieve a global lead in 3G devices. We had missed the boat on 2G, but we weren't going to let that happen a second time.

That was when I was appointed head of the internet dongle team. One afternoon in March 2006 Guo Ping, who was the CEO of Huawei Consumer at the time, had a talk with me. He explained what he wanted in a few brief sentences: "Internet dongles are a niche market. Company M and Company N aren't serious about this market, because it's small. I want you to head our internet dongle team, and the company will expect you to take a big chunk of the market. The goal here is to make healthy profits, for at least the next two years, and ultimately until the time when our phones start to become profitable." Having received my instructions, there was no backing out. The only thing to do was to overcome all difficulties, and make it happen.

Ongoing innovation decides the shape of the new market

Huawei's decision to invest heavily in R&D for internet dongles was the result of careful consideration. By 2006, there were many 3G networks in operation around the world, but few people were using them. It was as though we had built a highway, but there were no cars to drive on it. Clearly, there was a gap that internet dongles could fill.

Most people then mainly used their computers or laptops to access the internet. Internet dongles are a way of connecting to the internet: they contain a card that is able to connect to a mobile operator's network, and can be plugged directly into the computer. This means that users no longer have to be limited by the need to plug in with a wire. They can get online any time, any place, making mobile offices a reality.

Laptop internet cards at the time generally used a standard called PCMCIA, and they were large and unwieldy. They had to be plugged into a special slot on the laptop, and they were only used by a very few people. It was a tiny market.

So, in 2006, one of our operator customers asked us if we could update the PCMCIA card into a dongle that would plug into a USB socket. The request was relayed back by the customer manager to our R&D department. Our technical experts took one look at it and said, "It can't be done. You can't get enough voltage through a USB socket." But where angels fear to tread, there are always fools who will rush in, and we definitely had some 'fools' in R&D who thought it couldn't hurt to try.

So there followed a year of solid effort by the Huawei engineering team, led by some of our core technologists like Wu and Zhang. Finally, they solved all of the technical difficulties, and produced the world's first best-selling USB internet dongle, the E220.

The development of the E220 involved two technological breakthroughs. The first was the first mobile data connection via USB interface. This single innovation expanded the dongle market by more than tenfold. The second breakthrough was zero-installation: the E220 needed no CD-ROM to boot up, so customers could just plug and go, anywhere, any time. This was a massive step up in terms of convenience and simplicity.

In 2007, the Huawei E220 appeared in European media as one of the most important new pieces of consumer electronics, alongside the iPhone!

This success showed the team that technological innovation was the key to delivering user-friendly products. The E220 had successfully introduced a USB interface, but there was still a wire between the unit at the USB plug, so it wasn't quite as easy-to-use as it could be. We started thinking: can we get rid of that wire?

At the end of 2007, the E170 was launched. It was the first internet dongle without a cable. It looked exactly like a flash memory drive, so many called it a USB stick. In 2008, we launched the E180, the world's first USB internet dongle with a swivel head. In 2009, the E5 was launched, the first of its kind in the world, offering internet connections over wifi.

Our models kept on looking better and better, and each one provided faster internet connections. We were able to benefit from Huawei's technological experience in building 3G networks to create high-quality, competitive dongles and get them out onto the market fast.

Sustained innovation meant that Huawei's dongles were able to win over European consumers, and our market share rose and rose. We had achieved the first step in our strategy, which was to take the lion's share of this small market.

Turning a negative into a positive

Once the E220 had launched successfully onto the European market, we set our sights on Japan. The team was brimming with confidence. We were a hit in Europe, and we thought Japan would welcome the product with similar speed. But fate had a surprise in store for us: Company E, one of our Japanese customers, responded to our very first dongle product with a complaint about compatibility issues.

We were shocked. We had carried out every test we could think of back in China, using our product with every computer, but there were no problems at all. Why was it now failing to work in Japan?

An investigation soon gave us the reason: Toshiba's local laptops were different from the ones they sold in China. Even when it was exactly the same model, there were still differences in the software.

We had actually sent an engineer to Japan before the launch to try our dongle in real Japanese computers, but there had been a series of misunderstandings, and the testing never actually got done. The first time, our engineer had gone to Japan's biggest electronics market, but was refused entry because he was wearing jeans. The second time he wore a suit, but his interpreter couldn't make it, and the assistants in the stores didn't speak English well enough to help him. So, in the end, we just ran the compatibility tests on Toshiba units sold in China, and as a result, we were stuck in this embarrassing situation.

When we realized that the problem was with the computers, Yan Lida, then head of Huawei Japan, stepped in to help the

R&D team in far-off Shenzhen. Yan organized the procurement of some Toshiba laptops, and had them shipped back to China, saving us precious time.

We worked around the clock on the solution. Company E's head of R&D flew out to China to discuss the solution with us. He arrived at 9 am and left at 9 pm that same day. In the intervening 12 hours, he never even left the conference room once. We had arranged for a nice meal at lunchtime, but he insisted on eating the same takeaway that we got when we worked through lunch ourselves. It was heartening to be partnering with someone who would work shoulder-to-shoulder with us like that, but it also ratcheted up the pressure on us.

It took nearly a month, but in the end we were able to analyse every aspect of the problem. The team was exhausted. Several times over that month, they discussed whether they would even be able to continue carrying on at the crazy pace we had set. Was it even worth it? But we got daily telephone calls full of encouragement from Guo Ping, the CEO of Huawei Consumer, who was in Japan talking to Company E. What he kept stressing, over and over, was that we had to turn this negative into a positive.

Company E had bought one of every laptop model available on the Japanese market, and were conducting their own tests. They were extremely comprehensive tests – they weren't going to allow even the slightest problem to persist. Their relentless pursuit of quality and detailed testing methods were a baptism of fire for the dongle team. But their strictness gave us our second wind.

One month later, the E227 was relaunched in Japan. Six months after that, it was Japan's top seller, overtaking the offerings from Company E's other Japanese supplier. Our quality specifications were head and shoulders above any other product on the market. Company E's head of R&D said to me, "I always thought that Japanese companies were the hardest-working companies in the world. Now I see that you've got us beat!"

Company E treated the E227 as a joint project between our two companies. The next year, Huawei was named Company E's sole supplier, and our shipments to Japan multiplied. We also helped Company E take a much bigger share of Japan's market.

Later, Company S, Company N and Company K all got in contact with Huawei, wanting to buy dongles from us. We also developed the E5, a new generation of internet dongle. The E5 won an award as Japan's best new mobile device and became ubiquitous, sold in every shopping centre in the country. Afterwards, almost all the internet dongles used in Japan were produced by Huawei.

This process helped our R&D team to see that even the slightest mistake in quality issues could mean the end for a consumer product, and our ability to turn a crisis into an opportunity depended critically on the trust and encouragement of our leadership. Our strong team spirit was forged during these times of crisis and hardship.

Global reach

At the beginning of 2007, the Huawei Consumer leadership sent word that they wanted the Huawei internet dongles to achieve 100% global market penetration. Wherever there was a 3G network, Huawei needed to offer a dongle that works with at least one local operator.

Achieving this goal would require customized hardware and software, because operators prefer to work with Huawei when Huawei offers services tailored to their needs. But customizing our products means additional quality risks, and would impact our efficiency. The dongle R&D team was only made up of a few dozen people. Customizing our product would mean late nights at the office – often not clocking out until after 10 pm – and there were nearly 100 new versions to be developed. It felt like an impossible mountain to climb.

I called everyone together to discuss how we could hit the target we had been assigned. We decided to assign some of our best R&D people – led by an expert – to develop tools that would make the customization easier, by giving us a modular design. This would help reduce the quality risks associated with customizing everything by hand for each new customer. One year later, more than 80% of the customization work could be completed using software tools. For that part of the work, we didn't need to do any additional coding, so the work went much faster and the quality risks could be easily controlled. By 2008, a team of about 50 R&D engineers was able to produce 400 different customized versions of our dongles within just one month. We were ready to address the challenge of delivering a dongle for every 3G network on Earth.

Once the R&D solution was in place, it was time to address production. If we did manage to develop 1,000 or 2,000 different products, our production lines would have to be adjusted each time we swapped from one to another. Efficiency and speed were sure to take a hit. I personally went and spent more than a month at our supplier's production facility working out exactly where the difficulties lay in manufacturing customized products. Some of the issues could not be resolved within the manufacturing environment itself, and needed us to make changes upstream. One aspect was that we needed better sales projections and production planning. Another aspect was that we needed to make changes to our hardware design, so that the manufacturers could be more responsive. I called in our hardware engineers to come and spend some time on the production lines. They analysed more than 100 different manufacturing processes, then adjusted their designs so that the shared elements and universal printed circuit boards were produced first, and the customized processes were backloaded into the final stages of the manufacturing cycle.

The redesigned product hit the market in 2009, and the manufacturers were ready to take on the challenges. Simply by adjusting the last three manufacturing processes, more than a dozen different versions of the dongle could be produced, to meet the needs of networks in more than 100 countries around the world. Our manufacturing was now nimble enough to serve our goal of 100% global penetration. By improving our technology, once again we had turned an impossible challenge into a tractable project. Solving problems in a smart and practical way is always our objective.

Today, ten years later, the dongle team has far exceeded the challenging targets set for it back in those early years. We have maintained our number one position in this small market, offering consumers the world's best products and services. We have built up a seasoned team, and in a world of smartphones,

Internet of Things, tablets, personal computers and cloud services, we have created opportunities to serve an ever-larger market of consumers. Looking back, I can see the path we have walked, each step clear in my memory. We are all proud to be part of the Huawei Consumer team!

The Customer Said There Was Nothing to Discuss

By Cao Wei

I learned of Guatemala from the map when I was a child. Back then, I wondered what this country on the other side of the Earth would look like. During the course of my work at Huawei, I found out everything I needed to know about it.

Despite the earthquakes that seem to take place every few days, Guatemala is a jewel of a country. It has been several years since I was first assigned to work there. It was a time of hard work, collaboration and achievement.

Fighting for scraps

In 2011, clutching my brand-new passport, I arrived in Guatemala, full of anticipation for the sun-kissed beaches of Latin America. I had only just finished moving into the company accommodation and was still struggling with jet lag when the capital had a little magnitude 5.8 tremor just to welcome me. It was a useful introduction to the warm hospitality of Latin America!

I was touched by this somewhat overzealous welcome. In turn, I fired up the PowerPoint slide decks that we had been drilling on in New Employee Orientation, and went knocking on the door of a local operator, hoping that they would be equally pleased to see me. As it turned out, they weren't quite so friendly, and my contact there gave me a 5.8 jolt when she revealed their negotiating position.

She turned very deliberately from the slides to her own desk, pulled open one of the drawers, and began pulling phones and marketing flyers out one after another, letting them fall next to the Huawei sample I had presented. Then she flashed me a professional smile, rose, and said, "If your prices are the same as theirs, you will receive an order from us. If not, then we have nothing to discuss."

I collected up the materials. The three leaflets on the top of the stack were from companies with no brand value of their own – they were as good as white label manufacturers. It was basically unthinkable that we should offer our products for the same prices as these players. The customer was giving me the cold shoulder.

I backed out of the office. On the way back, I brooded over the problem: why did this customer think that the only dimension we could compete on was price? We had a comprehensive supply chain, and a production capacity of a million phones per year. Why did the customer equate us with these unknown brands?

There were many factors at play, but we only had one goal: to survive.

I got together with our account manager, and we got into the detailed work. We went over and over the key questions. What exactly do Guatemalan consumers want? What exactly does our operator customer need? Every day, I discussed these issues with the locals who worked for us: from consumer affordability to consumer habits, from brand recognition to human curiosity, from procurement strategies to reckoning the local ranking of brands. Our conversations sometimes bordered on the philosophical.

HQ was in the midst of preparations to launch the new Huawei flagship phone. We had ads to place, so we delved into our very limited marketing budget and visited every major billboard that we wanted to rent. Would our advertisements be properly seen from every angle? Some of the props we wanted for our launch roadshow could not be manufactured locally, so we asked visiting colleagues to bring them over from China. And in the last couple of days, when we got the designs for the billboards, we went over them one by one, checking with our local team and their family members that the ads conveyed the brand in the way that we hoped.

Everything was ready. The sails were set. We were just praying for favourable winds.

After all these years, I can still remember how I announced our determination to win to the team before going in to negotiate with the customer for the last time: "We have put together an excellent launch strategy. If they don't sell, I'm going to put my hands in my pockets and buy them myself!"

Shortly afterwards, we emerged with our very first order from a Guatemalan operator for a Huawei flagship phone: 50 units of the Ascend D1, sold!

Quality counts

The first 50 became another 50, and the first 100 became another 100. Consumers at first tried it because it was something different, then because they loved it. Our product began to gain traction beyond the existing Huawei fan base, and we saw reviews appearing on social media, along with little groups of Huawei fans. But even as our word-of-mouth swelled online, our customer, the operator, didn't seem to be catching on. They were slow to restock, so sometimes users who wanted to choose Huawei phones were forced to take other choices. It looked like our new-found success might be stillborn, after all.

We were asking the operator what was going on. The consumers were asking the operator what was going on. The operator's failure to order enough units was cutting into our customer base day by day, and the whole team was burning with frustration. We started to quietly survey phone retailers, but at just that moment, the operator came back to us with a suggestion: they wanted us to cut our prices and offer them more rebates for high sales.

We finally got the story from a retailer. It turned out that one of our competitors was making a play for the Guatemalan market. They had brought out a new phone with the same specifications as the Ascend D1 – same processor, same memory, same camera, slightly bigger screen – and were selling it for just half of our price! It was no wonder that the operators and retailers were flocking to buy this new offering!

I remained confident in the product we had. It seemed to me that the competitor was trying to chase us out of the market. They were gambling that we would fold under the pressure. But there had to be some problems with a phone being sold at that price. We quickly responded in two ways: the sales team looked into this competitor's operations in the Latin American market, and I went straight to the store to buy one of these phones and try it out for myself. The strange thing was, from the moment I walked into the store to the moment I handed over my credit card, not a single person mentioned a warranty. There was nothing on the marketing materials. This was unprecedented for a phone being marketed as the company's flagship model.

There were only two possibilities. Maybe this competitor had made a historic breakthrough in manufacturing technology, and was going to destroy us with prices we could never match. Or they were taking a big gamble, eating the losses so that they could take a decisive market share.

It was crunch time. We had to make the decision: do we cut our losses, or tough it out?

Those years of hard work are now a source of happy memories for us, and there are plenty more tough challenges to come!

"Hold the line!" When it came down to it, we were unanimous. Our team was full of mettle, and our strategic projections supported our instinct to fight. There is no faking quality, and our products represented a decade of investment and hard work. In the end, the market would sort the sheep from the goats.

Sure enough, it was not long before reports of quality problems started surfacing. Our customer, the operator, cut its orders of this competitor phone, but they ended up wasting a lot of time and effort dealing with problems from the units that they had already sold.

It had been a baptism of fire for me in this new market, but I learned a key lesson from this experience: if you want to survive in the long term, you have to compete on quality.

Seeking a new operator customer

Serving just one customer is a recipe for gradual decay. The more entwined you get with your customer, the more anxiety you feel. At our customer's procurement conference in 2014, we asked the head of Huawei's consumer team in Latin America to bring the whole regional expert team to Guatemala to come and talk with our operator customer. The meeting was very cordial, with some substantive points being discussed in a positive spirit. It seemed as though some of the long-standing friction might actually be resolved. But after our colleagues from regional HQ boarded their plane home, the customer said, "Those problems are still problems. No more orders for now!"

I started to think, we seemed to be stuck in a position where our route-to-market – the telecom operator – had all the power. The fact that this operator was our only customer meant that we had no negotiating position. Maintaining a good relationship requires give and take from both parties.

Our sales had been growing steadily, but we seemed to have been laying traps for ourselves. It was time to try a new strategy. We needed to start working with a different operator, so that we had a better mix of customers.

But would this mean that our existing customer lost interest in us? Would they transfer their affections to someone else? Developing a new customer is a long process. Would another operator understand and appreciate us? I was in a state of acute indecision.

It felt like my first days in the new country, when I didn't know anything, and had to ask questions continually. I felt like I didn't know where to start with this decision.

"My friend, you are no longer alone. You have us all. We're a team!"

It was at times like this that I really fell in love with my team and the great people of Guatemala.

If we were worried about the response of our existing customer, we could quietly negotiate with the new customer before a deal was reached. We divided up our product range, and the team began the process of building the relationship with our new customer. Both the new customer and we did not want to rush into anything. We were both looking for a deal that would benefit both parties, and over the course of many meetings we built mutual trust, and looked for synergy. A few years later, I became the regional account manager, in charge of the relationship with this new operator across all of Latin America. This operator's Guatemala procurement manager recommended us to his colleagues across the region.

Our new customer's new high-end phone took the Guatemalan market by storm, swiftly garnering rave reviews. At this, our older customer became interested in expanding its partnership with us. By this point we had established a much stronger position, and were able to impose some basic discipline around our sales channels.

Brand building

The success of the two-channel strategy had left us hungry for more. Our sales channels quickly expanded to all of the local operators and distributors. But the next challenge loomed. Although we had opened up new sales channels, we weren't seeing much growth in their orders. In fact, our sales seemed to be stagnating.

The relationships with our operator partners seemed to be progressing normally. They placed orders and promoted Huawei products as necessary, and we gave them decent incentives. But there was no momentum in our sales. It was like we'd hit some invisible ceiling, and there was just no way to increase our market share. What would the solution be this time?

Of course, when the going gets tough, a good manager doesn't let worry infect his team. I talked with our local sales director, and decided to organize two days of team building for the whole team. Everyone would be able to share their ideas and fully relax.

This conference was a turning point in the development of the Guatemala consumer product sales team. With the sales channels having reached maximum, everyone finally came to realize that for our consumer sales to improve, we had to return to the fundamentals of the consumer market: consumer approval ratings are the key to being competitive in this market, and marketing was the way to achieve them. I went on Weibo to find advertising copies and translated them to give everyone inspiration.

Once we had got the right mindset, the advertising copies spread. The part of writing that we all enjoyed most was brainstorming over coffee to create slogans and taglines. We would compete in a friendly way to see who could come up with the catchiest or funniest lines. Once we got started, the ideas would come pouring out.

Inspired by other regional offices, we placed advertisements on the walls of many shopping malls in Guatemala with the slogan "Next is here." This was a response to an advertisement that one of the major competitors was running at the time. We also took out front-page ads in all the major print media, and put our slogan "We are already here" in front of everyone in the country. This was a direct response to a campaign by another competitor.

Our ideas may not have been the newest or best, but the marketing team's enthusiasm, while we were still a small team, was enough to maximize our impact in every sales channel.

Another visit to Guatemala

In 2017, sometime after I had left Guatemala, I had the chance to return during a business trip. I toured around all of my old stamping grounds, and was lucky enough to see the local launch event for the next Huawei flagship phone. The local manager insisted that I stay for the launch, because it was going to be very special.

I accepted his invitation and came to the launch event in a state of some confusion. It didn't look like anything special, though there seemed to be more staff from the operator. Perhaps after all these years working together, the operator had developed a really close relationship with Huawei.

Photography exhibition at the launch of the HUAWEI P9

The operator's procurement manager came over and welcomed me in Spanish, "Hola, amigo! Bienvenido a nuestro evento de lanzamiento!" ["Hello, old friend! Welcome to our launch event!"] She gave me a big hug, as is customary in many Latin American countries.

I realized that this whole event was no longer organized and paid for by Huawei, as they had always been in the past. This was an operator event, especially put on to celebrate the launch of the new Huawei phone as part of their own range.

I looked at the procurement manager, stunned at the scale of these changes. I remembered all those years ago, the first meeting I ever had with her, and the dismissive tone in which she had said to me, "If your prices are the same as theirs, you will receive an order from us. If not, then we have nothing to discuss."

When I reminded her of that, "We have nothing to discuss," she couldn't help laughing and repeating it with me.

But she quickly continued: "But we did keep on with our discussions, didn't we? And we proved to each other that we both have a vision and the ability to achieve it."

"Salud" ["Cheers"], I said.

"Salud!" she replied.

Those years of hard work are now a source of happy memories for us, and there are plenty more tough challenges to come!

25

Where is the Way Out?

By Ji Rengui

On 8 November 2018, a colleague forwarded me a social media message from one of our customers in France. The message read as follows: "Five years ago, I bought a HUAWEI Ascend P6 smartphone. My friends didn't understand my decision at all. I told them, one day Huawei will have a big billboard here at the Water Mirror (Miroir d'eau). Finally, that day has come. I'm proud that I have been a Huawei customer for five years."

The billboard was a large outdoor ad for the Mate 20 Pro smartphone at the Water Mirror in Bordeaux. This message gave a boost to our entire West European consumer team. I felt that all of my hard work over the past three years had been worth it.

Huawei billboard for the Mate 20 Pro at the Water Mirror, Bordeaux

Huawei's progress in the Western European consumer market can be traced back to 2005. The first product we sold here was a 3G wireless data card. It was a huge success and helped to open the door to Europe for us. At the time, we also sold phones, but most were white label phones which were sold as telecom operators' own brands. Customers might have been using our phones, but would never see the Huawei brand.

In 2011, we decided to make Huawei-branded phones. But progress was slow for several years, and we barely made a dent in the

Western European market. In 2014 and 2015, our Mate 7 and Mate 8 smartphones were blockbusters in the Chinese market, but they didn't sell well in Western Europe. Our market share in Western Europe was so low that we weren't even listed in market reports, and simply lumped into the 'other brands' category. It has only been in the last three years that we have started making an impact in Western Europe. Step by step, we secured a foothold here, and we have managed to earn the trust and love of our customers.

Turning the tide: The P9 becomes our breakout phone

In February 2016, I was appointed director of the Huawei consumer business in the West European Region. My first challenge was the P9 launch coming up in April. I asked myself, "Can we use this launch to turn the situation around?" Then I got a reality check: we didn't have a chief marketing officer (CMO), nor did we have retail managers or channel managers. I wasn't very confident.

One weekend, I invited Zirong, Song, and Lei for a brisk walk around the Südpark in Düsseldorf. We walked around the park ten times, which was nearly 36 km. But we still hadn't come up with a workable plan. In the evening we found a good restaurant, and, after enough food, we set ourselves an ambitious goal: the P9 would make our name in Western Europe, just as the Mate 7 had in China, and we would sell one million units.

To make this ambitious goal a reality would take serious action. We first wrote out a full list of the telecom operators and retailers in Western Europe. We then broke the sales target of one million down into sub-targets for each of the ten countries in our sales territory, after which we broke them down further into specific targets for each of the top operators and retailers. We drew up plans for key operations in marketing, promotions, channel management, retail and services, with deadlines and designated owners for each task. We even organized a rally to get the whole team fired up and to get everyone to commit to our target of selling one million units of the P9.

In March, as the launch date approached, the entire team was working nonstop. Many even volunteered to work on Saturdays. They used the weekends to visit retail stores, compete for sales to key accounts, attend training sessions, review recent operations, and give presentations on their experience.

Everyone threw themselves headlong into the work. The teams in our ten different countries learned from each other, iterated and improved, and developed action plans that were well-adapted to their local markets. Our hard work finally paid off. For the first time, our phones were placed in the stores of Western Europe's 62 biggest operators and retailers. Even at the flagship price of €599 for the P9, our sales exceeded one million units. This victory gave our team and our partners a much-needed boost in confidence.

We will become number one in Western Europe
Hiring people who believe that Huawei will win

It was a big success, but could we make it sustainable? We were not satisfied with small wins; we wanted to become the number one player in the Western European market. However, Huawei was still just a minor brand in the local market in 2016, and our capabilities were limited.

Our regional office didn't even have a brand management team, and the marketing expertise of our marketing teams varied from country to country. We just weren't a professional marketing organization yet. What's worse, we didn't have a lot of basic data, such as consumption habits of high-end consumers.

We had to find the right people with the right skills. Vincent Pang, then president of the West European Region, pointed out that we shouldn't sit back and wait for people to find us. We needed to reach out and actively seek bright minds. So, what kind of people did we need?

First, we needed to find people who believed that Huawei would become number one. Only people who believe that the future is bright will take challenges head-on and use every means available to reach their goals. We must be confident, then we will be able to find our way forward. Huawei may still have been an 'other brand' in Western Europe, but we set ourselves the goal of getting in amongst the top players, then ultimately winning the crown for ourselves.

Second, we needed people who had passion, experience, potential, and leadership skills.

Third, we needed people who could fit into Huawei's culture, valued teamwork, had an open mind, and could learn from their environment. They also needed the courage to experiment and constantly improve.

I started out looking for a CMO. After interviewing more than ten candidates, Andrew immediately stood out. I met with Andrew four times. The first time, Andrew peppered me with questions: What is Huawei's branding framework and marketing strategy? What are the roles of HQ, regional offices, and country offices, and how do they coordinate with each other? What is the size of your regional marketing team, and what is their budget?

The second time we met, I told Andrew that our goal was to become number two within three years, and number one within five years in Western Europe. I briefed him on our regional office's strategic plan – achieving sales of US$10 billion within five years. This seemed to arouse a spark of interest in him.

Two weeks later, we met for the third time. Andrew shared his thoughts on how the Huawei brand could overtake other phone vendors within three to five years. I felt that he had the confidence in Huawei's future that we wanted.

During our fourth meeting, we got down to details about the regional and country marketing teams, as well as issues with the organizational structure. At this point, I thought he was very likely to join us.

However, to my surprise, he turned down our official offer. There was something off about the whole affair, so I asked HR to have a talk with him. It turned out that he had been hesitant whether he could maximize his value at Huawei and whether he would really be given the trust and authority he needed to do his work. Upon hearing this, I asked Pedro, then director of our Belgium office, to talk to Andrew. They talked for more than one hour, and Pedro explained the opportunities he was given and the growth he had achieved at Huawei. Finally, Andrew agreed to come on board.

Andrew has been working very hard since joining Huawei. He gradually built up a professional marketing team that can take on difficult challenges. Once I had coffee with him, and as our discussion flowed from work issues to our personal lives, he told me that during 2017, one of his closest relatives was seriously ill. Things were very difficult for him, but the happiness and sense of accomplishment he gained at Huawei made up for some of the pains in his life. I was very touched by this story and by his dedication to the job. I also felt guilty that I hadn't noticed this earlier, so that I could have given him some support.

There are many Andrews in our West European team: Carmen in Spain, Gregor in Germany, Isa in Italy, Ana in Portugal, Winston at our regional office ... These wonderful people give everything they have to the job, and have contributed a lot to our growing market share and the rise of Huawei as a premium brand in Western Europe. Without them, we wouldn't have been able to refit every retail store in Western Europe overnight for a new product launch. We wouldn't have been able to get so close to our customers. Without them, we wouldn't have been able to tell the Huawei story that moves and inspires our European customers.

Trust and autonomy bring our vision closer
Doing business in the consumer market is different from the carrier market. To succeed in a consumer market, everything needs to work together as a whole. A single weak link can cause the whole chain to fail. For me, what this meant was that I couldn't do everything myself. I needed to delegate, so that managers in each country office would take action by themselves.

Brand marketing is a good example of this. In order to keep our brand image consistent, the West European Regional Office once required that all marketing campaigns be approved at the regional level. But this move actually just slowed us down and failed to achieve the desired effect. We then tried setting up a system where operations and marketing were managed at the national level, with a set of explicit rules and processes, and procurement centralized at the regional level. With this new system in place, authority to act is handed back to the country offices, so 95% of matters can be decided at the national level.

Now, the country offices feel that they have our trust. More authority means more responsibility, which also means more stress. The director of our French consumer team once told me that he was so determined to achieve big sales that it was affecting his sleep. Trust makes people more willing to take on responsibility. Winston, our West European public relations manager, volunteered to take on the role of marketing director for a country in addition to his existing duties. Carmen, director of sales in Spain, personally took on the challenge of boosting our premium sales. Isa in Italy started in retail, and ended up as manager of both brand marketing and retail. The list goes on and on. Of course, this hard work does not go unnoticed. Those who do the most for the company are given the promotions and bonuses they deserve.

Marketing builds bridges with consumers

A good product is everything

Huawei phones have many unique features, such as powerful cameras, AI, long battery life, and a chic design. They were selling well all over the world, but why was it so hard for us to sell in large numbers in Western Europe? My team realized that the problem lay with marketing. To sell a product, you first have to market it.

There is an idealistic saying in Chinese that if you sell good wine, customers will beat a path to your door, even if it is deep in the back streets. But the first lesson we had to learn was that this is not the case in modern consumer markets. Even the greatest products need advertising. The HUAWEI P20 Pro had a brilliant camera, but consumers didn't buy it until the professional image quality ranking site, DxOMark, gave an unprecedented Photo score of 114 points.

The second lesson was that marketing is not just about flexing our muscles and telling our consumers how powerful our products are or the great experiences they can deliver. We need to localize our marketing so that it matches local culture and wins the recognition and approval of local consumers.

The third lesson was that we needed to tell our brand story in a way that reflects its warmth and humanity, rather than just the cold tech.

Art that highlights the beauty of technology

In the last two years, a number of luxury brand campaigns have incorporated historical elements. For example, Louis Vuitton did a range of Van Gogh-inspired bags, and Gucci created a collection based on the Renaissance. In 2018, we planned a campaign called

"Sparking Your Renaissance" that would be implemented across the ten countries in our West Europe region and would show off the powerful camera on the HUAWEI P20 series.

Sparking Your Renaissance event

In Italy, we used our P20 Pro to take photos of models in homage to Michelangelo's The Last Judgment. We then posted the photos online, and invited everyone to take photographs that recreated their favorite classic painting. We would arrange for a high-quality print of any photos sent in to us, and then displayed these photos in a month-long exhibition in front of Milan Cathedral. At first, people didn't believe that a smartphone could create images as beautiful as paintings, but the HUAWEI P20 Pro did. The event attracted more than three million people, who got a first-hand experience of our slogan: Make It Possible. It was a great marketing campaign, because it really resonated with Italians' passion for art.

In Spain, we invited a renowned Spanish photographer to use the HUAWEI P20 Pro to take a photo of the Annunciation – one of Spain's most famous Renaissance artworks. It was an artistic expression of our 366 Day theme (the arrival of AI). The photograph was then made into an outdoor billboard at the Plaza de España in Seville.

This advertisement had an area of more than 5,000 square metres, setting a Guinness world record for the largest outdoor billboard. The spectacle was a sensation in Spain, attracting the attention of tens of millions of people. A senior journalist on Televisión Española, a national television broadcaster, commented that, "No foreign brand has ever been so confidently rooted in Spanish culture as Huawei."

To promote the AI functions of our P20 series smartphones, like low-light photography and 5x zoom, we planned a campaign for the summer vacation months of July and August. We encouraged everyone to capture the beauty of life using their smartphones during their holidays and then have these scored by the AI function of their P20 phones. More than 1.2 million users tried out the function. We released the photos on a well-planned schedule, so that our viewers followed as if it were a TV show. Our customers came to believe that anyone can be an artist.

The beauty of life on holiday

We needed to tell our
brand story in a way that
reflects its warmth and
humanity, rather than
just the cold tech.

The human side of technology

In Germany, Huawei made a video that went viral. It was about a young man who sees a strange animal while riding his bicycle in a forest. He takes a photo and shares it on social media, making the animal known to more people. Then more and more people become interested and search for it in the forest. In the end, someone finds it and takes it to a zoo, so that more people can go and see it. In the end, the young man feels guilty about taking this poor creature from its home. So, he deletes the picture and asks the zoo to set the animal free.

This video was less than 60 seconds long, but it was viewed over two million times. It showed the great cameras on Huawei phones, and also our commitment to fulfilling our social responsibility. We were asking people to think about one question: would we choose to catch an animal and send it to a zoo, or let it return to nature?

Germany may have a reputation as a high-tech culture obsessed with practicality, but we chose to highlight the human side of technology. Our marketing made our brand more meaningful to consumers. Our market share in Germany continued to grow, and the Germany Rep Office won Huawei gold awards in 2017 and 2018.

Antoine Griezmann, a football player on the French national team, is Huawei's brand ambassador in France. We made a video telling his story, which was also very interesting. The original idea came from a Hollywood movie. A man was born with a strange disease that makes him look blurry in every photograph. One day, this man sees his footballing hero, Griezmann, and takes a selfie with him. The Huawei camera's AI bokeh function is designed to blur the background and focus on the foreground, so for the first time ever, the man's image comes into sharp focus, and he is overjoyed. Thanks to strong marketing, P20 sales in France almost tripled in 2018.

At the end of 2018, Huawei and the European Union of the Deaf developed a mobile app called StorySign. This app uses image recognition and Optical Character Recognition technologies to translate text within children's books into sign language, helping 34 million deaf children around the world to read and study. We also shot a short video about StorySign, featuring a deaf girl. The girl wanted a gift for Christmas and Santa sent her a Huawei mobile phone and a book. With the help of StorySign, the girl could read. The joy of the girl at that moment touched many people. This video attracted 130 million clicks and views.

StorySign video

Tech brings joy and life

The British are famous for their dry humor, so our stories in the UK needed to be told in a humorous way.

Our UK team ran a creative marketing event when a certain famous phone maker launched its new model. They parked a juice truck next to the line where people were queueing up, with a juice icon designed to look like a battery. People lining up to buy phones could get a cup of juice for free. Of course, there was one particular kind of fruit that they couldn't offer, because it just doesn't have enough juice! The stunt was well received by the British. The BBC even gave us 65 seconds of airtime, commenting on how much they loved this idea.

In 2018, we launched the Mate 20 series. One of the most powerful functions of these phones is their AI. As part of our marketing, Huawei held a Rubik's Cube competition in the UK. First, users took a photo of their cube using a specially-made app. Then the phone would instruct them on how to solve it, allowing anyone to solve a Rubik's Cube in just six or seven seconds. This event was a big hit, and helped show off the intelligence of Huawei phones.

The UK Rep Office rapidly grew to become one of our top seven rep offices for consumer sales. I also managed to deliver on a promise I made to Richard Yu, CEO of Huawei's Consumer BG, that I would double our UK sales.

An intelligent experience in every use case

In his 2018 New Year message, Richard Yu said that in the next five to ten years, 5G, AI, and IoT would be increasingly common and that we are looking at a trillion-dollar consumer market. He also said consumers were looking for a brand-new experience, and that Huawei will continue with the strategy of an intelligent ecosystem for every use case and will become number one in many domains.

After years of hard work, Huawei's consumer business has made solid progress in Western Europe. Where we used to sell phones for ¥1,000, we can now sell premium phones at €1,000 euros. We have secured a presence in this highly-competitive, €30 billion market. This is an important first step for us.

Western Europe is one of the most vital and visible markets for global consumer brands. Looking into the future, how can we build an intelligent ecosystem for all use cases in Western Europe? How can we provide better experiences to customers throughout the entire lifecycle of their Huawei purchases? How can we better execute our global brand marketing strategy? We are striving to become the leader in delivering an intelligent experience across all scenarios. There are no precedents for this, and no models to follow. But I am sure that we will find our way forward.

26

Embracing an Open Mind to Build a Diversified Elite Team

By Ma Qingqing

Time has flown by. I've spent over 20 years at Huawei. From R&D to sales in the Chinese market and on to overseas markets, I worked in many roles before starting in Human Resources for the Huawei Consumer BG in 2014. In recent years, our consumer business has grown rapidly, and the difference between the B2B and B2C markets is presenting a huge challenge for the Human Resources team. Our whole team shares the goal of attracting top minds from different parts of the world to join us. By doing this, we are ensuring that there are no weak links in our business and are forging the world's most effective team.

As our founder and CEO Mr Ren said, "No one cares where a winner comes from. As long as you can bring us success, we are brothers in the trenches." More industry experts, fresh graduates and colleagues from other Huawei departments are joining our Consumer BG, and being promoted as they succeed. This helps our customer team rise even more rapidly and allows us to build an elite team that is open, inclusive and diverse.

Huawei veterans: dedicated employees are forever young

In 2015, the company called on managers and employees from other domains to join the Consumer BG to support its rapid growth. Thousands of exceptional employees from other departments have joined Consumer BG every year since then and, through hands-on experience, they have developed deep expertise in different consumer business areas.

Junsong was among the first employees to answer the call of the company and volunteer to transfer to Consumer BG. On receiving his application, I said to him, "Since you don't have much experience in the consumer electronics market, I recommend first joining the Consumer Business Elite Team to get some experience. As part of the company's Strategic Reserve programme, this Team is the cradle for the company's future leaders. If you join this programme, you'll be able to get training and hands-on experience at the same time. Are you interested?"

Without any hesitation, he completed his job transfer and reported to the Greater China Region of Huawei Consumer BG. He had worked at Huawei for 18 years. But when the programme started, he – like many other colleagues who were new to the consumer team – experienced just how hard it is to switch from one line of work to another. Many retail concepts sounded like a different language to him, but despite the fierce competition he found fun and motivation in the challenges and opportunities. During his several months in the programme, Junsong travelled to countless local retail and service stores, large and small. During this period, he made friends with many Huawei customers, in-store promoters and service personnel.

After completing the programme, he joined the Greater China Device E-commerce Sales Department. The going was tougher than he expected. He used to work with telecom operators, and the key to success was laying everything on the line for one big sale. But in the consumer business, he found that the big picture mattered more. The Greater China Region had adopted an O2O model that combined online and offline sales. This model was different from both traditional phone manufactures who relied on bricks-and-mortar stores and the new breed of online smart-phone brands.

How could he blaze a unique path for Huawei in the e-commerce market? This was an unprecedented challenge, but his hard work paid off. Junsong and his team focused on this one issue for more than a year. Along with his whole team, Junsong was able to apply what he had learned in the training and practice programme, and produced great results with online and retail channels that reinforced and supported each other. Online promotions began to break sales records. All these achievements led to his appointment as the director of his department, and the team he led won the company's Gold Medal Award.

For the nearly 200,000 dedicated employees at Huawei, moving from one job to another is nothing new. What they gain from these moves is not necessarily rewards but the opportunity to start afresh and learn again from scratch. This is what inspires us to remain as passionate as we were when the company was just a start-up. We remain eager to learn, and never give up. Each new position we hold is a bold step forward. Dedicated employees are forever young.

Industry gurus: I had a limited understanding of Huawei Consumer

Jason was an expert in the consumer sector, and we reached out to him since he had certain skills that we lacked. Two years ago, I met him during a business trip to his city, hoping to persuade him to join us. At that time, he knew Huawei by reputation only: loud but mysterious. In fact, mysterious is one of the most common words that people use to describe us. I urged him to experience the atmosphere at our headquarters in Shenzhen, but he didn't accept the invitation until one and a half years later. Taking one or two years (or even longer) to recruit a top expert is actually quite common for our team.

"Huawei is not what I thought it would be," Jason said. "The senior managers don't have chauffeurs. They just call a cab to get to the airport. The interview was more like chatting with friends. During the interview, we didn't just talk about the job I applied for. Every interviewer was really excited about what Huawei does, and I could feel their confidence in the future. When the CEO of the Consumer BG interviewed me, he noticed that I had a Huawei phone. At once, he turned into a customer service representative and demonstrated how the phone functioned and how to solve my problems." Through these chats, Huawei came to understand Jason more, and Jason came to understand Huawei more. "I gradually realized that we are kindred spirits," he said.

Ultimately, he accepted Huawei's offer. It wasn't just the opportunities he felt the job would provide; it was the little things that he noticed at the interview that impressed him.

Vincent is another expert who joined our Honor brand this year. During his engagement with us, he was really impressed by the persistence of our Human Resources representative Yang. "I told Yang that I'd be on a ten-day road trip to Daocheng Aden, and that we'd talk when I got back. But he reached out to me every evening during my trip," Vincent said. "Even after work, when he was at home or walking his dog, he would call me, and we'd talk until late into the night. He was very candid in our conversations. He talked a lot about the business routines in Huawei Consumer, and always gave me an objective view without sugar-coating anything. His explanations helped me see the big picture of Huawei's consumer business.

I still wasn't sure about joining Huawei, but the way he continually engaged with me made me want to learn more about the company."

In Huawei's consumer business, we have always emphasized that finding excellent people is a job for all managers, not just Human Resources. Samuel is a leading Chinese expert in a certain area of the consumer electronics market, and we first met at one of Huawei's product launch events. I invited him over to give him a closer look at our international platform and the tremendous opportunities we offer for career development. I also thought talking with Samuel would allow me to really see his perspective as a consumer.

As it turned out, Samuel and the Huawei Consumer managers felt like old friends when they first met. They talked at length about the products, sales and sales channels, and found that they all held the same views on many things. After the meeting, several other members of our management team met him individually to speak with him further and seek his insight. Samuel's interest in joining Huawei grew.

Regrettably, when Samuel received our offer, he didn't accept it right away. When he submitted his resignation letter to his old employer, they took immediate action to retain him. What his company did to keep him impressed us because it showed how much they valued talented people. In terms of attracting and retaining the best, we still have a thing or two to learn from our industry peers. But we believe that in the near future, there will be more Samuels who would like to join our company.

90s kids: our team has a bit of magic

The annual Huawei Sales Elite Challenges and software contests are an important channel through which we discover and attract outstanding graduates. When I presented awards to the winners, some of their remarks impressed me a lot.

Yong from Tsinghua University said, "I want to go overseas to help grow the local consumer electronics market, and to broaden my own horizons. It is impossible for me to do this alone. So I am eager to work with a big company."

"If I hadn't taken part in this competition, I never would have known how driven I could be," said Min, from Huazhong University of Science and Technology.

An atmosphere where young people can motivate and inspire each other has attracted many fresh graduates to Huawei's Consumer BG.

Yanxia is a financial news graduate from Peking University who is now working in the Huawei app store team. She signed up with us as a graduate in 2016. She is a millennial and she shares many of her generation's typical qualities: she likes sharing her views, wants respect for her individuality, does not like being told what to do with no explanation and thinks independently. She has shared some of her thoughts on joining us: "I am fortunate that Peking University, with its diverse and inclusive atmosphere, helped me develop independent thinking and an adventurous spirit. I felt even happier when I knew that I could hold on to my individuality after joining Huawei. My mentor Hua has really embraced that in coaching me."

Launching apps is one of Yanxia's most important duties. From day one, she was given opportunities to take on challenging tasks. During her third month with the company, she was already launching apps independently. Just after passing her probation assessment, she released more than 20 apps herself, eight of which immediately went to number one in their own niche stores. Giving our young hires trust and authority enables them to learn and mature quickly. Yanxia has now accepted a new challenge to boost engagement with post-millennial users.

Yanxia was fortunate that her mentor set a good example of how to mentor newcomers. In recent years, our management team has frequently discussed how we can help those in their early twenties quickly integrate and unleash their full potential while respecting their individuality. There is still a lot of room for improvement in this area and, as we see it, the power of exemplary employees will help even more outstanding young people stand out. It is only in this kind of atmosphere that young people are able to maximize their value, constantly innovate and fearlessly push beyond their limits.

To Yanxia, Huawei was like another university, and the new employee orientation was like another freshman orientation. Senior managers from Huawei's offices around the world explained Huawei's business and culture to new hires. The experience of selling products and providing services in physical retail stores helped Yanxia understand how Huawei's corporate culture of customer-centricity is practised day to day. During the one month

she was in stores, she wore a Huawei T-shirt and quickly mastered
the basics of Huawei phones, tablets and other consumer devices.
She enjoyed the process of speaking with hundreds of consumers.
At the end of the training, Yanxia said a sad goodbye to the group
she had been trained with, as they went to their new jobs in all corners of the globe. They took with them not just a new understanding of their work, but a freshly minted Huawei family.

Awards ceremony for the Huawei Sales Elite Challenge

At Huawei we remain focused on the work, and don't let ourselves get distracted. Everyone likes to follow this straightforward
approach and to stay professional in the workplace.

Retaining young managers with career development and opportunities

Many people are curious about what kind of person succeeds at
Huawei. Peter Hu is a young manager who has rapidly risen in the
ranks at Huawei Consumer. He has been with the company for 11
years, and spent ten of them outside China. I would like to quote
what he said here: "Our consumer business started from nothing
during my first days in the overseas markets, but it had lofty ambitions. I have been able to develop because the company trusted me
and gave me the freedom to succeed."

Peter started as an entry-level product manager, but within three years he was promoted to country manager. In just seven years, he became a regional director of Huawei Consumer business. They say that the best leaders come from humble beginnings and work their way up. Huawei insists on developing, assessing and promoting managers based on their real-world work experience. We also move people across different regions and departments as their career advances. In Peter's words, "The chance to take skills for different jobs is the best incentive."

Ten years of hard work overseas earned Peter a Diligence Award, with his family attending the awards ceremony. The best part of any journey is the things you see along the way. Peter gained experience with different nationalities, different cultures and in different parts of the world as he worked in southern Europe, NCEE and then sub-Saharan Africa, and these are the treasures of his life. After all, happiness is a life full of good memories.

Peter has now returned to Huawei's HQ and is working as a manager. He has witnessed the full story of Huawei Consumer, from customizing phones for carriers to creating our own consumer products, and I am sure that he will bring a lot of business experience from the field to his new managerial role at HQ. The constant flow and mobility of our employees and managers is another reason why our team remains vibrant and energized.

Eastern and Southern Africa consumer team meeting Huawei fans
(Johannesburg)

In terms of attracting and retaining the best people, capacity building and team development, Huawei Consumer still lags behind the industry's best practices. We still have a long way to go. To build an elite team that is truly ambitious, effective and inclusive, we must stay hungry, keep learning and improve quickly.

Huawei Consumer BG is eager to work shoulder to shoulder with anyone who is bold, smart and passionate, so that we can continue to complete many more missions impossible!

Editors

Biography of
Tian Tao

Tian Tao is a member of the Huawei International Advisory Council, Co-Director of the Ruihua Institute for Innovation Management at Zhejiang University in Hangzhou, China, and a Visiting Fellow at Cambridge Judge Business School.

In 1991, Mr Tian founded *Top Capital*, the first Chinese magazine on private equity investment, and has served as Editor-in-Chief since.